IMPRINT

Caitlin Press Inc.
8100 Alderwood Road, Halfmoon Bay, BC V0N 1Y1
www.caitlin-press.com

Text design and cover design by Vici Johnstone
Printed in Canada

Caitlin Press Inc. acknowledges financial support from the Government
of Canada and the Canada Council for the Arts, and the Province of British Columbia through the British Columbia Arts Council and the Book
Publisher's Tax Credit.

Library and Archives Canada Cataloguing in Publication

Sicherman, Claire, author
       Imprint : a memoir of trauma in the third generation /
Claire Sicherman.

ISBN 978-1-987915-57-0 (softcover)

       1. Sicherman, Claire. 2. Sicherman, Claire—Mental health.
3. Sicherman, Claire—Family. 4. Grandchildren of Holocaust
survivors—Mental health. 5. Holocaust, Jewish (1939–1945)—
Psychological aspects. 6. Psychic trauma. 7. Intergenerational
relations. I. Title.

RC451.4.H62S53 2017   616.85'210092   C2017-906074-0

IMPRINT

a memoir of trauma in the third generation

Claire Sicherman

CAITLIN PRESS

For Ben

"What is done cannot be undone, but one can prevent it happening again."

—Anne Frank

My maternal grandparents were survivors of the Holocaust and I am their legacy. Every day I make a choice to keep creating new narratives for myself and to live my life in their honour, in the honour of all survivors, and in the honour of all those who perished in the Holocaust.

There is an urgency to the stories of our survivors. My grandparents have passed away. Their voices were silenced, and when they were finally free to tell, they lost their ability to speak about the horrors, about the stories that were too hard to share. These remain buried. I may not have details of their trauma, but I carry their experience in my body, the violence transmitted through me, imprinted, and so it is from this third generation perspective that I write. Writing is one way of giving voice, of remembering, of processing, of grieving, of creating meaning and of healing.

This is for you, my babi and děda.

I love you.

My Family

Klára Lebenhartová
Babi's mother. My great-grandmother. Born March 1, 1883. Deported from Prague to Theresienstadt via Transport AAu, No. 808, and arrived in Theresienstadt on July 27, 1942. On August 4, 1942, Klára was deported via Transport AAz, No. 704 to Maly Trostenets in Belorussia. Klára was gassed. The exact date of her death is unknown. She was 59.

Richard (Rída) Lebenhart
Babi's brother. My great-uncle. Born October 27, 1914. Deported to Theresienstadt from Prague via Transport Di, No. 518, and arrived in Theresienstadt July 13, 1943. On September 6, 1943, Richard was deported to Auschwitz via Transport Dl, No. 1208. He was gassed on March 8, 1944. He was 29.

Hana Lebenhartová
Babi's sister-in-law, married to Richard. My great-aunt. Born June 23, 1920. Deported from Prague to Theresienstadt via Transport Di, No. 517, and arrived in Theresienstadt July 13, 1943. Deported from Theresienstadt to Auschwitz on Dl, No. 1207, September 6, 1943. She was gassed on March 8, 1944 at age 23.

Bedřich Bloch
Děda's father. My great-grandfather. Born September 9, 1871. Deported from Klatovy to Theresienstadt, September 26, 1942, Transport No. 257. On April 12, 1943, he committed suicide in Theresienstadt.

Hedvika Blochová
Děda's mother. My great-grandmother. Born February 28, 1879. Deported from Klatovy to Theresienstadt via Transport Cd, No. 258, November 26, 1942. Deported from Theresienstadt to Auschwitz on Transport Et, No. 1349, October 23,1944. Date of death: March 1944. Murdered in Auschwitz. Cause of death unknown.

Marie Lípová
Děda's sister. My great-aunt, born Blochová.
Born July 30, 1902. Deported from Prague to Theresienstadt on Transport Au, No. 420, May 12, 1942. Transport Ay, No. 481, May 17, 1942 from Theresienstadt to Lublin. Murdered. Cause and date of death unknown. No one survived from this transport.

František Líp
Děda's brother-in-law, married to Marie. Born July 6, 1899. Deported from Prague to Theresienstadt via Transport Au, No. 418, May 12, 1942. Deported on Transport Ay, no. 479, May 17, 1942, from Theresienstadt to Lublin. Murdered. Date of death: August 13, 1942, in Majdanek.

Kity Lípová
Děda's niece. My cousin. Daughter of Marie and František.
Born December 12, 1929. Deported from Prague to Theresienstadt via Transport Au, No. 419, May 12, 1942. Deported on Transport Ay, No. 480, May 17, 1942 from Theresienstadt to Lublin. Murdered at age 12. Date and cause of death unknown.

Anna Blochová
Děda's sister. My great-aunt. Born December 4, 1911.
Deported from Klatovy to Theresienstadt via Transport Cd,
No. 259, November 26, 1942. Deported from Theresienstadt to
Auschwitz via Transport Eq., No. 204, October 12, 1944. Murdered. Date and cause of death unknown.

More family members who perished in the Holocaust:
Rudolf, Eliška, Vilém, Karel, Rudolf, Marie, Anna, Julius, Max,
Julia and many others whose names we don't know.

BOOK ONE

"The preservation and transfer of memory is the most critical mission that children and grandchildren of survivors must undertake so as to ensure meaningful and authentic Holocaust remembrance in future generations."

—Menachem Z. Rosensaft
God, Faith & Identity from the Ashes: Reflections of Children and Grandchildren of Holocaust Survivors
Jewish Lights Publishing, 2015

"The concentration-camp experience represents an evil so appalling that we too, when we turn to face it, suffer psychic unbalance. We too flounder in nightmare, in a torment having nothing to do with us yet felt in some strange way to be very much a part of our deepest, most secret being. The terror of the camps is with us."

—Terrence Des Pres
The Survivor: An Anatomy of Life in the Death Camps
Oxford University Press, 1976

December 5, 2015

Dear Ben,

Even though our family remains silent, our bodies hold language that tells us we are grieving. The hunched backs, the curved spines, digestive problems, nervous systems that won't stop. We hold heaviness in us, a constant mourning for the dead. The body carries fragments of memory, it inherits loss, it senses the presence of ghosts, it hoards the ends of loaves of bread in the freezer *just in case.*

There are Holocaust books all over our kitchen table. Sometimes I turn the books around so the spines are hidden to make sure you won't read them. Other times I leave the books with their covers in full view, hoping you will see them and ask me the question: *Mom, what is the Holocaust?* You are nine years old. Although I am waiting for the question, I don't know how to talk about it with you. Not yet. But I know it's a conversation we must have. Although it isn't easy to share the truth, remaining silent only brings suffering.

A good friend of mine suggested I start with a letter to you as a way of writing about our family. You see, Ben, I am feeling overwhelmed about writing our story down. It's overwhelming because we know so little about what happened. About your great-grandmother, your babi, and your great-grandfather, your děda, about the rest of our family, and your dad's family too. The other thing is there's so much death, so much trauma. How do I go about writing such things without getting triggered myself?

Over the last few months, I've felt so sad. This sadness runs deep, and I am grieving. But I'm also having a hard time crying. And I've heard so much about the benefit of having tears, about the cathartic release they can bring. And when those tears get stuck, it means I'm stuck. I'm stuck, Ben. I'm writing to tell you this. I'm frozen in a state of overwhelming sadness.

I'm scared, too. I'm scared to give our ancestors a voice. Scared that I won't do this voice justice. And scared that if I don't try, I will forget about them. And I can't do that. I won't do that.

I am not going to forget our ancestors and I'm not going to let you forget them. Their stories will live here on these pages, in the hearts of those who read, but especially in mine.

Love always,
Mom

IT'S THE KIND of winter sun that shines cold. The hazy kind. The kind where the sky is a mass of foggy grey with only the slightest hint of a white fuzzy ball. The kind that offers no warmth, but makes your insides freeze instead.

I am at home writing. I left work early because I feel like my body is bursting to tell. *Her* story. Klára's story.

Is it weird to be named after someone who died? I ask the question because I'm not sure. I'm not sure how much of her hangs over me like a heavy wool blanket, creating my narrative for me.

My entire family thinks she was shot in the back of the neck at the edge of a dark forest in Belorussia. It's a story we have come to believe because we don't know. When we don't know exactly how someone dies, when we don't see the body, when we can't pick up the ashes or dig out the grave. When there is no headstone, or piece of rock, or even a stick. When there is no conclusion. Then we'll believe anything.

In the cool prickles of the pale winter sun, I Google Maly Trostenets, a concentration camp in Belarus, and find the transport she was on.

August 4, 1942.

I find that instead of being shot in the back of the neck, she is stuffed into a van filled with gas, and when the van reaches the edge of the Blagovschina Forest, she is already dead.

My nine-year-old son comes home from school ten minutes after I learn the truth. After I learn about how my great-grandmother really died. Ben's cheeks are red, his curls soft, and when he sees me he smiles, and drops his backpack on the floor. He attacks me like a football player, tightens his arms around me and presses the side of his face against my chest. I smell the top of his head and wonder if he can hear my heart thudding—if he can sense what I have just learned.

Journal Entry #1

Wikipedia tells me that *necronym* is derived from the Greek words *nekros*, dead, and *onoma*, name.

Dead name.

It's an honour to be named after someone who died in the Holocaust. For many Jews, it's tradition to do so. It's even considered a mitzvah, a good deed. It's a way of remembering the dead. It's also thought that the soul of the deceased will continue to live on in its namesake.

Klára and I. We share the same name. We're connected. Her spirit is bonded with mine.

What Google doesn't tell me is how being named after the dead can feel like a burden. How I carry the weight of my great-grandmother's suffering. How her death will be forever fused with my life.

WHEN MY GREAT-GRANDMOTHER, Klára, was fifty-nine, she was murdered by the Nazis.

I was named after her.

Emphasis is placed on the first *a* in her name, and it's long and flat and rhymes with Ma. The long *a* makes her sound regal, otherworldly, a moment captured.

I type her name in Google. The first thing I see is a Wikipedia page about Klara Hitler.

I freeze. And then I read it.

Wikipedia tells me she was quiet and sweet and affectionate. That she had six children but only two survived to adulthood. That when she died of breast cancer, Adolf carried this grief with him.

After I read about Klara Hitler, I close my laptop. I sit and listen to my heart thump in my chest and reverberate in the rest of my body.

I can't feel anything.

On August 4, 1942, Klára Lebenhartová was put on a train with a thousand other Jews from the Theresienstadt ghetto outside of Prague and transported over six days to Maly Trostenets in Eastern Belarus. Forty Jews were selected for hard labour. Klára and 960 of the deportees were ordered off the train, forced to hand over any valuables that still remained with them and undress. They were then crammed into large vans that looked like moving trucks. One van could hold approximately one hundred prisoners. Gas vans were machines of mass extermination that had air-sealed compartments designed to kill people via engine exhaust. There was a tube connected to the exhaust, and when the driver turned on the motor, it was death to the prisoners by carbon monoxide poisoning.

What was it like to be a driver of such a van? To sit in the front seat in neutral gear, the motor running for ten minutes, amidst the screams and the pounding, the clawing and the gasping? Would the driver casually light a cigarette? Would he tap his knee to some imaginary beat and hum along? Would he roll down the window and yell at his buddy, something funny, a joke maybe, and they'd both laugh?

After ten minutes, when it went quiet, the drivers would shift gears and they'd drive the vans to the edge of the Blagovschina Forest. When the Nazis unlocked the doors to the vans, they had 960 dead bodies to dispose of.

My great-grandmother, my Klára, her body was thrown into a pit.

It is estimated that sixty-five thousand Jews were murdered at Maly Trostenets. The Soviets found evidence of thirty-four mass graves in the Blagovschina Forest. I find a picture of it online. Everything is alive, green. There are pine trees, birch and oak. There are shrubs and grass and moss. In the middle, between trees, it looks as though there is a clearing. Underneath the photo, the caption reads, "The Execution Site at Blagowshtchina Forest near the Maly Trostenets concentration camp."

I am anxious to relay this new information to my parents and to my husband, Jeremy. No one in my family knows what happened to Klára's transport. The Nazis had bombed Maly Trostenets and destroyed records in order to hide evidence of genocide. This is the first bit of information we have.

My body is a tightly coiled spring, and I ricochet around the kitchen with tears in my eyes, a fear-hole in my stomach.

I think about Klára's son, Richard, my babi's brother, and his wife, Hana. They too were gassed and died from asphyxiation. They were murdered at Auschwitz with Zyklon B, a gas previously used as a pesticide. A gas designed to kill rodents and insects.

This is what happened to Klára: she was asphyxiated, her red blood cells filling with carbon monoxide. It's called the silent killer because it's invisible and has no odour. It takes only a few minutes to die.

The Mayo Clinic tells me the symptoms of carbon monoxide poisoning are as follows: dull headache, weakness, dizziness, nausea or vomiting, shortness of breath, confusion, blurred vision, loss of consciousness.

I learn that in Greek asphyxia means without pulse.

My mind wanders to Ben.

Nine years ago when he was born, the word asphyxia was written on his hospital report.

THERE IS A WIKIPEDIA PAGE on gas vans. Gas van or gas wagon. *Not to be confused with gas trucks*, the Wikipedia page instructs. Before I find out my great-grandmother was murdered in one, I didn't know gas vans existed.

Turns out even the Nazis were getting a bit stressed out from shooting so many women and children. They needed a more efficient, less messy way of killing large numbers of people. So they found it: gas vans and gas chambers.

Wikipedia tells me gas vans had two disadvantages: death came slow and the screams of the victims came loud.

JEREMY, BEN AND I take a walk in the forest on Galiano, a southern Gulf Island near Vancouver. Douglas fir, western red cedar, hemlock. We reach a path where the trees grow thick and dark. Layers of swordfern and salal. Ben is nervous here because the light is dim. His face twitches and his ears pick up a raven's song. We continue walking and come across a large hole that looks freshly dug. I think of my Klára, my great-grandmother, my namesake. How large was the pit where her body was thrown? How many bodies were piled into mass graves? Were some people still alive when their bodies were tossed like bags of garbage? Was Klára's body flattened with a tractor and covered with dirt to hide the evidence? Or was she burned, cremated in the pit? The music the Nazis played from the gramophone as they were executing people, German military-style march music, unrelenting, whipping into frenzy, blasted through a loudspeaker? A scream is said to activate the brain's fear centre and is designed to scare those who are listening. Did this march music make it easier for the Nazis to kill people? Did it help drown the noise of Jews screaming as they were murdered?

LAST NIGHT I SPOONED with my great-grandmother. Six hours have passed since I found out how she died. Ben is nicely tucked into bed. Jeremy is out with a friend. I know to stop reading about the Holocaust. I remember my rule about not scaring myself before bed. But the evidence calls to me. I walk down the stairs even though I am frightened to open my computer. And I read. I read again about Maly Trostenets, about the Blagovshchina Forest, about Klára's transport, about gas vans and carbon monoxide poisoning. And then I wonder what is the better way to die? Digging one's own grave and then getting shot in the back of the neck? Or stuffed into a sealed van and suffocating on poisonous gas?

Was Klára hysterical? Did she claw at the sides of the van, struggling to get out, or did she sit in stillness, breathing it in, calmly accepting her fate while the bodies of others smashed into hers?

I spend an hour reading alone in the shadows of winter. When I am done, I close my computer. My insides shake. I get up and stand on tiptoes and turn on all the lights.

I walk over to the wool rug and feel the small nubs, like pebbles, under my feet. The fireplace glows red, and above, the large smiling moon face carved out of cedar. Jeremy's grandmother's piano that I don't play sits by the window next to the beige couch. An album cover sits on the plastic top of a record player. Without looking, I know it's ABBA's *Greatest Hits,* my son's favourite.

I am safe. I am safe. I am safe. I am safe.

While I brush my teeth, while I wash my face, while I check on my son and tuck in his covers, I say these words. I say these words while my heart thumps as I put the dirty laundry in the hamper, while I shut the lights but keep the one in my room on, while I put on my fleece socks and curl up under the duvet.

I am safe. I am safe. I am safe.

This is when my Klára, my great-grandmother, my name-sake, comes to me. She is ethereal and the light from my room shines right through her. Like a parachute descending from the sky, she floats down from the ceiling and wraps herself around me, a blanket, soft and smooth. I turn off the light and she spoons me with all her love and warmth, and she stays with me as I drift off to sleep.

December 12, 2015

Dear Ben,
Have you ever had a dream that keeps haunting you? Like the one where your family of humans transforms into a family of goats and then a giant—like the evil one from "Jack and the Beanstalk"—comes, and there are flames shooting from a massive pyre, and this giant takes your goat family and throws them into the pyre, one by one, and all you can do is watch them burn, and then the giant looks at you and you know it's your turn.
Have you ever had a dream like this?

Love always,
Mom

THIS IS *HER* STORY about survival. My grandmother, my babi, who is over 102, is dying. A survivor of the Holocaust, a survivor of the communist invasion, a survivor of life as a refugee, a survivor of her husband's suicide.

A survivor of a broken hip at 90. The other hip broken a few days ago.

She didn't want to go this way. Lying in bed, barely there but breathing, whites of eyes, moving hand to face.

"Let me just fall asleep and never awake," she used to say. "Not like my father who died of a brain tumour, or like my mother and my brother who were murdered by the Nazis. Let me go in peace."

My 102-year-old babi is fiercely proud of her independence. "It could be worse," she told me when she moved to the Lodge just before she turned 100. "I can still stand, dress myself, walk."

My mother shows the nurse my babi's Auschwitz tattoo. The nurse runs her finger over my babi's number.

72540.

"She is so strong," the nurse says. "We get a lot of survivors in here."

My mother found an article about how genocidal trauma is associated with longer lifespan. It says survivors' resilience and courage, along with their physical and mental strength, contributed to their longevity.

My babi, who survived the Holocaust, the communists, life as a refugee, her husband's suicide, a broken hip at 90 and another at 102, survives a second hip surgery.

She is conflicted about death. She often tells me she wants to die. But there is another part of her that wants to live.

The drapes are open and the Vancouver city lights shine through. I am standing beside her hospital bed, holding her hand. It is dry and cold. The skin on her fingers is tough like leather, but on her arms it's so thin I can almost see through. Her hair, which she always wore in a neat bun, has come loose.

"Cross your fingers and toes for me," she says before her surgery.

After her operation, the nurses try to put her in a wheel-chair. My babi can't do it. It is agony. Pain rips through her body.

They give her drugs.

—

"Babi had a stroke last night," says my mother. "She didn't know we were there."

Her voice on the phone sounds small, hollow like a shell.

My breath catches. "But how?" I begin. "I don't under-stand."

"They're going to keep her comfortable," she says.

There is so much I want to talk about when it comes to my babi. The truth is, I don't know most of her stories.

What I do know is that she is a survivor.

I owe her my life.

She is stronger than anyone I know.

On these pages, in my heart, she survives.

IN PRAGUE, EVERY STEP feels old, as if being transported into a fairytale. A Hansel and Gretel type story, but in Czech instead of German. Things don't look real. The buildings are bright and cheerful in *Staré Město*, the Old Town, each one a different colour and shape. They look fake, part of a movie set. The cobblestones, the clock tower, the castle, the bridges, the winding streets that lead nowhere and everywhere, opening and closing in rhythm of the river, the mighty Vltava, undulating through. A city of young lovers, of poets, of musicians, of art. A city full of Jewish relics, spared only because of Hitler's vision of a museum to showcase the extinct race.

On March 1, 1936, in Prague, in *this* fairytale city, the city where my grandparents were born, my babi and děda are married. They get married on Klára's birthday. My babi carries a bouquet of white lilacs. My děda holds a pair of tan leather gloves. For their honeymoon, they travel to northern Italy to visit the lakes. As my grandparents return from their trip, my děda buys Hitler's *Mein Kampf* for the journey home. "It certainly wasn't an entertaining read," my děda writes to his cousin in Seattle, "and certainly not appropriate for newlyweds who were returning to their new home in Prague to start a life together." But like many millions of European Jews, my grandparents believe Hitler won't last. They think he's a joke. There are no thoughts of fleeing. My babi and děda won't leave their families behind. They are citizens of Czechoslovakia, and my děda and my babi's brother, Richard, served in the army and swore to protect their country. Leaving was for the weak and unpatriotic.

On March 15, 1939, the German army marches into Prague. When my děda travels to visit his parents in Blatná, a town in Southern Bohemia, the shop window of his father's store displays a sign: *Jüdisches Geschäft*, Jewish Shop. By summer, the prohibitions have begun, with Bohemian and Moravian Jews required to relocate to Prague and carry identity cards; they are restricted from frequenting restaurants, playgrounds, theatres and hospitals, along with many other institutions, all of which hang signs saying: *No Jews.* Jewish children are prohibited from attending school, and by 1941 Jews are restricted in what they can buy to eat, are barred from going for walks in forests, have their phones disconnected, and are forced to wear a black-outlined yellow Star of David marked with *Jude*, the German word for Jew, in Hebraic-style lettering.

The purpose of the badge is to humiliate and ridicule by marking Jews as pariahs. Jews have to purchase the badges, cut stars out of coarse yellow cloth and sew them on the left side of their clothing, sometimes on the back and the front. The penalty for not wearing the badge is paying a fine, imprisonment or death.

In September 1941, Hitler gives the position of Reich protector to Reinhard Heydrich. In three months, thousands of Czech people are arrested and hundreds executed. In November 1941, in the old fortress of Terezin, Heydrich establishes the ghetto and concentration camp Theresienstadt, which serves as a holding camp for Czech Jews waiting to be deported to the death camps in the east. It's Heydrich who begins the deportations of Czech Jews in 1941. It's Heydrich who deports my family to the horrors of genocide.

What must it have been like for my babi and děda, for the millions of others, when the world was eclipsed by evil?

When November comes I can feel the shadow of my grandparents' suffering, as if it has found a home in my body, bewitching my mood, a chronic sense of foreboding. In the heavy gloom of the winter months, the tension in the bodies of my babi and děda, their nerves extra prickly, picking up any sound outside, a dog barking, the wind's haunting summon through a cracked open window, the crunch of thick black combat boots.

I don't know how they are taken.

I imagine a sharp knock on the door in the middle of the night. My babi and děda sit up in their bed. They've been waiting for this moment. Caged in their own home, they know what is coming. Two nights ago their neighbours were taken away. The door is kicked open and they hear shouting, *"Juden Raus!* Jews get out!"* German Nazi soldiers burst in looking like angels of death in their black uniforms, brandishing clubs, black swastikas dancing on their red armbands.

I picture this scene in my head, but I also imagine one where my grandparents receive an order to vacate their apartment and appear at the Trade Fair Hall just outside of Prague, with their fifty kilos of luggage. They have been slowly giving things away, leaving some money and a few valuable items with trusted friends. Their bodies are rigid, the cold and damp of December enters and never leaves.

On December 22, 1942, my grandparents take a tram from Prague across the river to the Trade Fair Hall. There, they are herded together like animals with thousands of others, the same hall I visited when I was a teenager, the same hall where I sat down to watch a concert, Smetana's majestic *Vltava*, a symphony that echoes the movements of the great Czech river. The longest river in the Czech Republic, it is often referred to as the national river. And though it meanders peacefully in places, there are parts that are wild, untamable rapids. When I listened to the music, the hairs stood up on my arms, and I shivered and cried.

Relieved of the keys to their apartment, their identification cards, their money and valuables, stripped of their personhood and tagged with numbers they are forced to wear around their necks, my babi and děda walk in procession to the train station where they board a train to Theresienstadt. As the train begins to move, they watch their lives vanish, replaced with the violence of those in charge.

Journal Entry #4

Bad posture is my body's way of protecting itself. With a nervous system that is always running, it stays tense and contracted. In the bleak dullness of December, the month of my babi's birthday, the month that my babi and my děda were deported to the death camps, I sit hunched, my shoulders slump, rounded back, my arms hang low, my knuckles almost scrape the floor, my whole body in mourning. If I allow myself to keep holding this posture, the one that I've held for forty years, my body will continue to suffer and my pain will continue as chronic.

My grandmother always hated her birthday. Whenever I wished her happy birthday, she would scoff and flap a hand across her face, scowling. I thought maybe the reason was that she was old. But that wasn't it.

I can't remember when I learned the real reason she hated her birthday so much. My babi was born on December 18, 1911. Four days after my babi's thirty-first birthday, on December 22, 1942, she and my děda were deported to Theresienstadt, a prison infested with lice and vermin, with little access to water and food. On the exact date of my babi's next birthday, December 18, 1943, she and my děda were transported in sealed cattle cars from Theresienstadt to a death camp—Auschwitz. It is the site of the largest mass murder in a single location in human history.

How dark were those darkest days, how black were the nights.

December 18, 2015

Dear Ben,

Two black bears wander through a woman's yard in Vancouver's north shore again. I read it in the newspaper. She hears her dog barking. When the dog's voice goes hoarse she knows there are bears. They barrel through the alley in the dusk of winter. They get into trouble. They knock over garbage cans. They leave their prints and their vomit and their big bear scat. They leave chunks of fur on the metal fence post.

These bears used to hibernate in the dead of winter.

Like me.

The stuff that we bury always comes back up.

—

My body comes alive in the winter. In the oppressive grey of December, my babi and děda are deported to Theresienstadt and the following December, taken to Auschwitz. The curve in my spine folds my body into itself and I often find myself lying on the floor, listening to the ghosts, my insides frozen but the rivers of my veins, the oceans from within, a constant flow—my blood no longer red, but the bluest blue of an iceberg.

—

Your ears are like two large satellite dishes, it's like they rotate to pick up the slightest of frequencies. I watch your body go rigid. "What was that?" you whisper. We listen alert like animals, listen when the winds prick the trees, the cracking, the shaking, the shivering of green. Together, our spines are rigid and our hearts drum. You grow like this in the depth of my love, in the swaying branches of our ancestors.

—

I never really knew I had a body. It was like this dead weight I carried around. Except that it wasn't dead at all.

Love always,
Mom

December 22, 1942: My babi and děda are transported on Ck476 from Prague to Theresienstadt. A relative who was already in Theresienstadt pulls some strings and my děda manages to get a job in the bakery, which means the family has bread.

December 18, 1943: My babi and děda are transported on Ds-2073 from Theresienstadt to Auschwitz.

July 1944 to March 1945: My babi is transported from Auschwitz to a subcamp near Hamburg called Neugraben. Her job is to clear rubble after allied bombings.

1944 to April 1945: My děda is in Schwarzheide and Sachsenhausen concentration camps. He labours in a quarry and climbs up ladders, carrying slabs of stone.

March 1945 to April 1945: My babi is in Bergen-Belsen.

April 15, 1945: My babi is liberated in Bergen-Belsen by British soldiers. She is dying from typhus. There are piles of corpses; the ground is alive with lice. Sixty thousand survivors, most in critical condition due to the typhus epidemic. Twenty-eight thousand die in the weeks that follow.

April 22, 1945: My děda is liberated in Sachsenhausen by Soviet troops. He is dying from tuberculosis. There are only three thousand prisoners left in the camp—my děda along with the others who are too weak to be sent on a death march. On April 20 and 21, thirty-three thousand prisoners are evacuated by the Nazis and forced to march on foot. Those who are unable to keep up are shot. Many starve to death. Thousands die.

THE NAZIS BRANDED PRISONERS so they could identify the bodies as they died. It's commonly referred to as a tattoo, but the prisoners had no choice. In Auschwitz, my babi's arm was branded, like livestock, to prove ownership, to reinforce that her life didn't belong to her.

The single needle was soaked in ink and the numbers were punctured into the flesh of my babi's left forearm. In the Jewish religion, it is forbidden to mutilate the body.

My babi's number, 72540, was a nice round number that when repeated aloud sounds like someone's home address. I punch her number in Google. Apparently it's the best place to live in Guion, Arkansas.

The tattoo occupied the soft of her outer forearm, skin wrinkled so paper-thin it was translucent, veins flowing blue. My babi would wear long-sleeved blouses, which covered up her tattoo, but every so often her sleeve would inch up and the numbers would poke out. During our Scrabble games or lunch, my eyes were drawn to the blue-black ink.

My babi wouldn't talk about the death camps. But she'd point to her tattoo. She'd show it to me as if she was proud of the way it was a solid line, perfectly straight.

"I saved my bread," she would say. "As a bribe to the prisoners in charge of tattooing, so they would make my numbers look nice."

She doesn't tell me that other prisoners, like her brother, Richard, and his wife, Hana, were never branded like she was. Six months after their arrival in Auschwitz, arms naked, they were gassed to death instead.

I recently thought about getting a tattoo. Nothing big. Probably a word. On my left inner wrist. Small and cursive. But I'm having doubts. If I seriously think about it, my stomach twists into snakes. I recoil. I know this fear. It blows deep into my belly like a foghorn. Then comes a feeling, disgust or horror, and my brain shoots to my grandmother's perfect round number.

72540
72540
72540
72540
72540
72540
72540
72540
72540
72540
72540
72540
72540
72540
72540
72540
72540
72540
72540
72540
72540
72540
72540
72540
72540
72540
72540
72540
72540
72540

January 3, 2016

Dear Ben,
When you hear German, do the tiny hairs in your ears bristle? Do you wonder what the Germans were doing when your family was murdered? Whether they were complicit in their death?

Love always,
Mom

MY FAMILY LOVES BREAD. Most kinds. Even the squishy white bread that has no substance or nutritional value. When I go to Vancouver's Granville Island market with Ben, instead of whining for a cookie, he asks for a baguette and then walks around gnawing on the end. No butter. Just plain.

My freezer is full of bread. The bottom is so stuffed with bread there's no room for anything else. These aren't whole loaves either. These are fragments. Bits and pieces, odds and ends from last January. Seriously. I usually end up composting them, although my mother would be horrified to hear this. She'd take those pieces and eat them herself, lest anything go to waste.

My mother has bread in the freezer. My sister, Leah, has a freezer full of bread too. I don't know what happens with her bread. I don't ask.

My grandmother loved bread.

In my family, a meal isn't complete without a good piece of rye, with butter spread an inch thick.

In Auschwitz bread was like gold. The stale piece a prisoner was sometimes given was often gobbled up. A few times when my děda hid his piece of bread beneath his thin mattress at Schwarzheide concentration camp, it disappeared during the night and he'd have nothing for breakfast to go along with the chicory coffee, or black mud as he called it. Other times it was carefully saved and used as a bargaining tool, a way of trading. I think of my grandmother, who stood in line for her prison serial number, using her piece of bread as leverage to ensure her tattoo looked nice, that the numbers were straight, that the ink didn't bleed. The bread that was supposed to go into her starving belly went into someone else's stomach instead.

Journal Entry #9

The Ten Plagues of the Death Camps:

I. Jaundice
II. Lice
III. Scabies
IV. Starvation
V. Typhus
VI. Tuberculosis
VII. Dysentery
VIII. Diphtheria
IX. Typhoid fever
X. Death of the First Born, and the Next Born, and the Next...

IN THE DEATH CAMPS, my babi made sure she went to wash every day. She remembered an old rusty tap, near the latrines, that dripped dirty water. She walked a long way to that tap. She knew if she gave up washing, she would be giving up her life.

My babi lived on her own until she was ninety-nine. She had a routine. She woke up, did her exercises and washed. Every morning she'd stretch, and slap her body Shiatsu-style. She wanted to stay mobile, keep fit. She didn't want to move into a care facility. At that time, she hadn't stepped foot outside her apartment in years. She never took the elevator to the main floor. She'd even stopped venturing out onto her balcony.

In August 2011, my babi's toilet started to leak and water seeped through the floor and poured down into the neighbour's apartment below. My babi couldn't hear the neighbours as they frantically knocked on her door. My babi couldn't see the water as it flowed from her toilet. My babi's neighbours called my parents in a panic and my mother and father cancelled their plans and rushed over to help.

My Mother's List For My Babi

October 2011

Dear Matinko,
With deep regret here is a list of reasons why you can't live on your own anymore.

1. Last Sunday your neighbours were banging on your door and calling you by phone. Did you hear them?
2. Who will the neighbours call when something else happens in the future and we may not be home?
3. How many people do you know who live on their own once they reach one hundred years?
4. You say that you are my small child now. How many small children do you know who live on their own?
5. I know you'd like to stay here until you die but unfortunately it's not possible. You can't hear, you don't understand what people tell you and don't remember what's going on around you.
6. You have to also take into consideration your family and your neighbours who get worried and have to drop everything as soon as something happens to you here.
7. You have never been selfish and I hope that you will understand that you cannot stay here any longer for selfish reasons.
8. You used to tell us that it's up to us to decide when it's time to move you to an old-age home. Regretfully, it is our decision that the time has come.

líbá, tvoje dcera (kissing you, your daughter),
Jana

MY BABI WAS ALWAYS OPEN to the possibility of moving into an elderly care facility when my parents deemed it necessary. In October 2011, my babi moved into the Lodge. I wait two weeks before I visit to let her settle. The street is lined with large maple trees and there are benches and a concrete fountain in front. I stand beside the rhododendron bushes and stare at the park across the street, watching some sort of curly doodle dog chase an orange ball. The owner talks on his cellphone and carries a blue plastic ball launcher that he uses to swat at the ground as he walks. When the receptionist sees me through the glass doors, they slide open.

My babi's room is 326. There are four floors that go according to cognitive capabilities. The first and fourth are reserved for those residents who are higher functioning. The third floor is one step below. And then there's the second. When the elevator doors opens, there are people sitting in wheelchairs mumbling to themselves or sleeping. A woman with a guitar and a warm smile sings, "You Are My Sunshine." A man tries to clap along. Two verses behind, another woman sings, "Please don't take my sunshine away."

One morning when I visit my babi, she's in the middle of doing her exercises. I ask her if she has eaten yet and she says she hasn't.

"This is the nicest prison I've ever lived in," she says. "How ironic that I've been starving most of my life, and now that I have no appetite, I have all this food to eat."

My babi doesn't talk about the war except to tell me about her parents and her Auschwitz tattoo. I listen even though I've heard the story many times before. She feels sad about the way they died. She says that even though her father died from a brain tumour, he was lucky because he didn't have to bear witness to the destruction of his family.

Of her immediate family, my babi was the sole survivor.

Journal Entry #18

I've visited Theresienstadt three times. It was the transit concentration camp-ghetto that imprisoned my family before their deportation to the death camps. Out of the 140,000 Jews who were sent here, 90,000 were sent east to killing centres. Each time I visit, it's late spring or summer, and the green of the grass and trees interrupt my grief. In places, it smells like rotting things and sewage. The quiet adds to the heaviness, a dreary grey that hangs despite the sun. I remember walking through as if I had been hit on the head, unable to process.

Here is a disinfection station designed for the delousing of prisoners and clothing. Here is a railway line built by prisoners with transports leaving for Auschwitz. Here are the barracks used as a hospital. Here is the attic that housed a secret prayer room. Here is the cellar where prisoners were taken and never returned. Here is a crematorium built by the Nazis to dispose of the dead bodies.

Over 35,000 prisoners perished in Theresienstadt. Starvation. Disease. Exposure. Forced labour.

The ghetto was created to fool the rest of the world while the Nazis continued the extermination of six million Jews and millions of others: LGBTQ+, Roma, people with disabilities, people with mental illness, anyone of African or Asian decent, sex workers, Poles, Russians, Serbs, Freemasons, Slavic people, Spanish Republicans, members of any political opposition and resistance, Jehovah's Witnesses, Roman Catholics, Protestants, Baha'i, Esperantists, Ukrainians, Czechs, Greeks, communists, socialists, repeat criminal offenders and many, many other people.

Jewish artists and intellectuals were deported to Theresienstadt and the Nazis sold this model ghetto to the Western allies as a cultural retreat. When the International Red Cross came in June 1944, the Nazis prepared for their visit by intensifying the deportation of Jews to death camps in order to "clean up" the ghetto and minimize overcrowding.

I remember art on the walls drawn by children. Butterflies, flowers, mountains and the moon contrasted by ashen barracks, fierce guards, electric fences, a wagon wheeling away dead bodies.

There was poetry too. My mother once gave me a book called *I Never Saw Another Butterfly*, a collection of drawings and poems by children who were imprisoned at Theresienstadt. But I never read it. It's still sitting on a shelf behind a closed cupboard door. Just the thought of opening it makes my heart break. Of the fifteen thousand children deported to Theresienstadt and then to death camps, less than one hundred survived.

I remember the amount of art that came out of that place, a place of such violence, the beauty that comes out of death.

In 1994, my sister and I visit Theresienstadt for the first time. When we are done, I take a piece of red brick from the dusty ground and place it in my pocket.

January 11, 2016

Dear Ben,

When we used to visit Babi, after she moved into the Lodge, we would call her first from the phone downstairs beside the fish tank to announce our intention to visit, as to arrive unannounced would make her anxious. My babi didn't like surprises. I don't know if this has anything to do with the death camps, the way prisoners were barked at by the guards, the way they were woken up whenever the guards felt like waking them, the way they were beaten if they didn't move fast enough. My babi needed some notice, even if it was only a few minutes.

"Hi Babi, it's Claire," I would say.

"Claire," she would reply, her voice thick with sleep. "Thanks for calling."

"Can we come for a visit?" I would ask.

"Of course. When?" she would say.

"In five minutes?" I would answer.

"Okay," she would say. "That's fine."

Then we'd gather around and watch the fish dash back and forth in the tank. The clown fish would hide in the pink fingers of anemones while the yellow tang would show off in front, charging around the brain coral.

"Look at that blue one," you would say. "It's swimming in circles. Does it know it has nowhere to go?"

After five minutes, you pushed the button, calling the slow elevator up to the third floor.

When we reached her room, we knocked even though my babi was mostly deaf and couldn't hear it anyway. But it was courtesy, as was the call announcing our visit. When we opened her door, my babi would be seated on her green chair in the corner by the window. Her room sat across from the park and she could see the branches of the trees. She was happy to have the trees. They reminded her of the mountains she left behind when she moved out of her apartment in West Vancouver. My babi slept upright in her chair most of the day, preferred this to lying down, although she did sleep in her bed at night.

"Benny," her face lit up when she saw you. "So nice of you to come visit your old babi. *Pusinku na čelíčko*, a little kiss on your little forehead."

You walked straight to her and offered her the top of your head to kiss, as you always did when you were little.

I opened her drawer and rummaged for her pocket talker, a hearing device with headphones attached to a cable that had a small black box and a wire connected to a microphone. I placed the headphones over my babi's ears and then switched it on and when we spoke into the microphone, she could hear us.

I leaned over and kissed her on the cheek.

"How long has it been since I've seen Benny?" my babi would ask.

"About three weeks," I would say.

"Really? It feels like longer," she would say.

I grinned. By now my family and I were used to answering the same questions from Babi. At 102 years old, she had short-term memory loss and would often repeat herself a few times during a visit.

You and I would each pull up a chair and sit as close to Babi as was possible. She also couldn't see well, so proximity helped. In her room my babi had a TV she no longer watched, a clock she could no longer see and a phone she could no longer hear. On the desk, there were old pictures of our family, ones of Leah and me when we were young, and photos of you when you were a baby. There was nothing on the walls.

I knew not to ask Babi how she was doing because her answer was always the same: "I wish I were dead, but it could be worse. At least I have my brains and my health. I can walk without assistance and get dressed on my own. Not bad for 102." Then she'd talk about her parents and how they died and she'd ask me if she had told me the story before. I would shake my head no and listen even though I had heard the story many times before.

My babi would sit and ask you about school, what subjects you liked best, what sports you played, how tall you were. You'd sit and answer for five minutes before your body started to twitch and you'd turn to me, your eyes imploring, "Can I leave now?" After a few more minutes, you would pass me the microphone, hop off the chair and give Babi your forehead to kiss again. Then you'd zip out of the room and ride the elevators up and down, up and down, until I was done.

Love always,
Mom

Journal Entry #21

I don't remember when I first learned about the Holocaust. It feels like I have always known about it, that I was born knowing bits and pieces of my family's story. That despite the silence, my body was aware of these fragments much earlier than my mind could comprehend.

In 1993, on Christmas Day, my family celebrates by watching *Schindler's List*. It's opening night and the theatre is packed with Jews. After, because it's tradition and because it's the only restaurant open on December 25, we go out for Chinese food. Even though no one is hungry, we order too much food. A steaming plate of noodles looks like greasy worms. Pieces of orange chicken drowning in a bloody sauce. Egg swirl soup, pale and drippy, makes my stomach turn, and the beef and tomato fried rice looks like guts, spilled out. We stare at our plates.

A year later, the Vancouver Holocaust Education Centre opens its doors with an exhibit on Anne Frank. My mother and I volunteer as docents and we each receive a mug with Anne's face on it. I feel a connection with Anne, as if she were part of my family. When I move out on my own, I keep the mug in a cupboard high up where I can't see it. Later, I find out my babi was in Bergen-Belsen at the same time as Anne. They both contracted typhus. Anne died just shy of her sixteenth birthday, approximately a month or two before liberation.

I REMEMBER MY BABI'S HAIR being soft and grey and tucked away neatly in a bun. Just before bed, when Leah and I slept over, she would let her hair down, and I was always surprised to see the smooth silver cascade down past her shoulders. When we slept over, my sister and I would fall asleep in my babi's room, and then Babi would join us later.

I never saw my babi cry but I do remember her sadness. She didn't laugh a lot, or even smile, and when she did, her hand would dive to cover her mouth. She didn't like having visitors, didn't like people in general, and she worried a lot. Before I got married, she worried so much about having to see people at our wedding that her hair fell out. She came anyway but wore a navy blue headscarf.

My babi was a no-nonsense grandmother. She was firm and strict, the Eastern European stereotype. When she gave me and my sister a look, she meant business.

Here is what my babi liked:

1. Strong coffee.
2. Discussing politics.
3. Rummage sales.
4. Reading fiction and biographies. (She liked reading about American presidents and read a very thick biography on Harry Truman. She also read books in German and French. In between non-fiction, she'd read Harlequin romances.)
5. Knitting us clothes and blankets.
6. Languages. (English was her fourth language after Czech, German and French. She read books in all four and took a French class at the community centre.)
7. Her daily walk to the library, where she'd tear the crossword puzzles out of old newspapers and take them home to finish.
8. Scrabble. (She was so good she used to get impatient if we took too long to put down words.)
9. Baking. (She'd bake a pie or cake for us every Sunday when we came to visit. She used to watch us eat and her face would light up and then she'd wrap up the leftovers for us to take home. She made Vánočka—a Czech braided bread with raisins—and also plum cake, apple crumble, chocolate cake with icing and crepes.)

It was spring when the light returned and the bodies who survived were liberated. At the end of the war, my grandparents were both so ill that neither cared if they lived or died. My babi with typhus and my děda sick with tuberculosis in Schwarzheide. As the allied bombing intensified, and they witnessed the bodies of their friends being blown apart, my grandparents lay dying in the barracks, too sick to move away from the danger. My děda was pronounced a *Muselmann* by the camp doctor, a term used by the Nazis to identify prisoners in the concentration camps who were ghosts—skeletons waiting to die. Instead of being forced on the death march like many of his friends, my děda was excused by the camp doctor due to his illness. Then he went to sleep. Only when my děda was liberated by the Soviet troops did he open his eyes again, and he was taken to a hospital in Prague. He did not know the whereabouts of his wife, my babi, whether she had survived or not. He did not yet know the fate of his family: he did not yet know that aside from my babi he was the sole survivor.

After liberation from Bergen-Belsen in April 1945, my babi was put on a Red Cross hospital ship and sent to Sweden, where many schools had been temporarily converted into hospitals, to recover from typhus. My babi weighed only seventy pounds. With food and rest, she slowly recuperated. In August, an official from the Red Cross came to see her, and when my babi mentioned her last name was Bloch, the official told her my děda was alive, although sick, in Czechoslovakia. He then told my babi that she was the only member of her family to survive.

January 24, 2016

Dear Ben,

When I drive by the smokestack at Vancouver General Hospital, I picture the crematoria in the death camps, the large furnaces that burned the bodies of our family along with the millions of others who were murdered.

In the summer, when I drive you to drum lessons, our windows open wide, we pass by a poultry factory. It smells like all things dead. When the winds blow west, we wrinkle our noses and I wonder what the camps smelled like. Did the people who lived nearby get used to the smell? When they hung their laundry up to dry, did they stop and think about the incineration of entire families, the millions who were turned into ash falling from sky?

Love always,
Mom

IN NOVEMBER 1945, my babi returned to Prague to reunite with my děda. They hadn't seen each other in over a year and a half, since being forcibly separated in Auschwitz.

My babi and my děda, almost dead, allowed themselves to heal, but the scars never left them.

To begin again. How did people manage to begin again? How does any survivor of horrific trauma begin to live again? What did it feel like to come back knowing one's entire family was murdered?

I imagine the startled looks on people's faces when they saw my grandparents were alive. These people saw two ghosts. I imagine parts of them wondered why they were not dead, like the rest. I imagine them imagining what my grandparents must have done to survive. I have read about how people were irritated by the return of the survivors, now skeletons, faces gaunt and ashen, constantly searching for family and friends who may have survived. I imagine other people didn't understand, could not comprehend the magnitude of what happened. I imagine my babi and my děda felt incredibly lost. This feeling must have been so unbearable they had to bury it to keep going.

After filling out stacks of forms and standing in endless lines, my grandparents secured an apartment with some money they had left with trusted friends before their first deportation to Theresienstadt. A German family had previously occupied the apartment during the war but had since vacated and fled back to Germany, and before that the apartment had belonged to Jews. Their old apartment was not available anymore, probably given to a German family or simply taken over by locals during the war. My grandparents had stored some personal belongings with friends and managed to get some items back to furnish their apartment. A Persian rug, their old wooden chairs and table, monogrammed napkins from their wedding. A few of their belongings never returned to them. One night when they visited their friend's apartment for dinner, the tablecloth from my grandparents' wedding was on display. My grandmother never said anything.

So they lived.

They cobbled together a life among the ghosts and they didn't talk about the nightmare of their shared experience, as if the hell they had lived through belonged to somebody else.

Less than three years after one brutal regime, my grandparents were forced to live under another. In February 1948, there was a putsch, and the communists took firm hold in Czechoslovakia. My grandparents and their Jewish identity remained hidden behind an iron curtain, a regime that didn't tolerate any kind of identity except for one that supported the communists. Anti-Semitism was raging and Jews were associated with capitalism, imperialism and the West.

On June 20, 1949, my mother was born and my grandfather finally got the child he had always wanted. My babi never wanted kids. She thought the world was too dangerous for children.

"Babi was pregnant before the war started," my mother said. "She never told Děda about the abortion. She told me after he died. She knew Děda wouldn't have agreed with it."

My mother said my babi spoke to her about it in a factual way, as if she were reciting her list of things to do. She told my mother that she went to her doctor and got it taken care of. She knew it wasn't safe to bring a baby into the world. That with Hitler, and his plans for war and the attacks against German Jews, starting a family was a bad idea. That my babi would have been sent to the gas chamber with her baby, just as other mothers with their babies had been.

Journal Entry #25

I am walking with Ben in the city one cold, crisp winter morning. The sun makes the sidewalks sparkle as the seagulls float above the clear blue sky. He is nine years old and round, rosy-cheeked, and he reaches his right arm straight up but at an angle. He holds it there and continues marching and I don't tell him to stop because *he doesn't know*. He is still innocent, still unaware about the Nazi salute and goose-stepping. I am triggered with an image of grade six. I'm on the playground field again, the boys with swastikas pinned on their cadets' uniforms, goose-stepping, arms outstretched with their cries of "Heil Hitler!"

THERE IS AN ABSENCE in my knowledge. Spaces, gaps. Memories that don't exist. This absence is called silence. Silence when my grandparents returned to Prague and continued living without addressing the horror they had both survived. Silence. No one spoke about the family members who were murdered, whose lives were stolen, whose bodies disappeared, dates and location of death unknown, again and again.

How did they die? Who saw them go?

Silence when my mother was born, an effort to fit in, to not draw attention, to keep safe. My mother playing with a bunch of kids outside her apartment block, ugly beige stucco peeling, identical copies stamped all over the city. A girl, Dasha, three years older, gets mad at my mother and runs upstairs. She pokes her head through the hole in the winding staircase and squints her eyes and spits, *zhidovka*. My mother doesn't understand that Dasha just called her a Jew. She doesn't know that word, has never heard it before. My mother believes Dasha called her *uzhovka*, which means snake.

My unknowing mother enters her apartment on the second floor and stays silent. Then when my babi gives her a bath, my mother tells her story.

"Why did Dasha call me a snake?" my mother asks.

"Why did she use the word *zhidovka?*" my mother asks.

"What is a Jew?" my mother asks.

BEFORE MY MOTHER was born, my babi and děda changed their last name so they wouldn't be easily identified as Jews. They got rid of *Bloch*, and instead chose *Lípa* in honour of my děda's sister, husband and daughter, Marie, František and Kity Lípa, who were murdered in the Holocaust.

Every September, my babi baked a large loaf of bread, which my grandparents called *barches* (a braided bread known more commonly as *challah*). This was also the only time my děda bought grapes, as fruit was not easily accessible under the communists. My babi and děda shared one glass of white wine and děda mumbled words in a language my mother didn't understand. They cut the *barches* and ate a few grapes. My mother was never told about Rosh Hashanah.

She didn't know they were celebrating the Jewish New Year.

In early December, my babi and my děda arranged for a small gift to be given to my mother on St. Nicolas Day. On the sixth of December, a devil, bishop and angel came to their building and knocked on the door. When my mother opened it, the three spirits asked my grandparents whether she had been a good child. My babi and my děda answered yes or no. One year, my mother got a lump of coal and a little doll.

Christmas was celebrated on December 24 and it was tradition to eat carp, which my mother hated. They had a Christmas tree because it was safer that way. They hid their Jewishness in the decorations, the candles, the handmade paper chains. At the top of the tree sat a shining star.

After decorating, my babi and my děda sent my mother out of the room so they could put gifts under the tree. One year my mother remembered how excited she was to get a doll in a buggy. Every Christmas, after opening her presents, my mother was treated to a single orange, which she shared with her parents.

My mother was told these presents were from baby Jesus.

Journal Entry #29

An article in the news recently reported that incidents of anti-Semitism in Canada have increased over the last decade, along with a rise in Holocaust denial. Last week a large black swastika was spray-painted on a bus shelter outside of our apartment building. I saw the city worker trying to scrub it off. I noticed the right angles of the swastika reach out like black spider legs. And I have a flashback to grade six when the boys in my classroom used their drafting tools to slowly carve swastikas into their plastic binders. The cool boy called my name and when I looked over he pointed his sharp tool at his red binder so I could see all the hooked crosses. I averted my eyes and looked down at my desk, my head hanging low, my eyes blurred with tears. It's then that I saw the outline of a tiny swastika scraped into the hard plastic.

IN POST-WORLD WAR II Prague, anti-Semitism was rampant. Many Jews were accused of conspiracy against the Communist Party and lost their jobs, were imprisoned and executed. Synagogues and churches were closed or demolished. Their neighbours knew my mother and grandparents were Jewish but my mother didn't know how they found out. She wasn't friends with any Jewish children. She didn't know anyone who openly identified as a Jew. She still didn't know what being a Jew was.

When my mother was a teenager in Prague, she worried about dating. Should she mention she was Jewish? Would anyone want to go out with her?

"In Děda's library I found a book about Auschwitz called *Death Factory*," my mother told me. "I read it in secrecy and learned about the Holocaust. I didn't ask my parents any questions. They never found out that I had read it."

When my mother was young, she spent two weeks every summer in Radešovice, a small town outside of Prague. My babi's parents owned a modest summer home made of brick, located on the main road leading to Prague. The home had gardens out the front and back with a stone fence around the property. There was no running water and my mother remembered pumping water in the backyard and carrying the buckets up two flights of stairs. The toilet stank, as there was no flush, only a bucket with water to rinse it out. Once my mother was horrified to see two large fat worms wriggling in the ceramic bowl.

Next door was the summer home of my babi's cousin's family. Before the war, it was a place where the extended family would gather: kids, parents, cousins, grandparents, aunts and uncles. After the Holocaust, my babi and my děda filed paperwork documenting their ownership and it was returned to them. Except there was no extended family left to gather. It was just the three of them. And sometimes it was just two, when my děda took my mother on his own.

It was in Radešovice that my mother learned how to swim. On her way to the lake, which was more like a muddy pond, she crossed through a forest of fir trees. There were spaces between the trees, not like the dense forests of British Columbia, and she walked through the forest with my babi, who was a great mushroom hunter. Together they picked boletus, chanterelles and shaggy mane, and my babi would make a mushroom and egg omelet for lunch.

The water was warm, brown and murky, like a dirty bath. A kind, old man, who was a self-proclaimed swim instructor, held a pole that rested on a wooden beam. The pole had a long rope attached to it, and at the end there was an inner tube. In shallow water, my mother would climb through the inner tube and the old man would move the pole over the beam and carry my mother through the water. Tipped forward with her body in the inner tube, my mother learned how to do the breaststroke. The kind, old man would teach kids, one at a time. My grandmother stayed in the shade, embarrassed by her figure, which she considered fat. Only my děda occasionally swam with my mother.

Later, when my mother was older, she sunbathed on the grass. She slathered baby oil over her body to ensure the deepest tan, and her skin would burn and blister. A few days later, her friends would sit in a circle and peel the skin off her back. My mother said it felt like a snake shedding skin.

Sometimes my mother went to Radešovice for a day trip with my děda. They didn't have a car so they took a tram, then a train, and walked the thirty minutes from the station. The garden was ripe with red currants, prune plums, cherries, apples and pears. My děda and my mother would fill two large bags each and carry them thirty minutes to the train, then to a tram, which would eventually take them to their apartment in Prague. My babi would be angry when they brought the heaving bags of fruit back home because it meant she'd have to spend time canning, on top of all the other work she had to do. Canning and drying the dishes were the only chores my děda would help my babi with. The rest he called "woman's work" and left for my babi and mother.

When the Persian rug needed cleaning, my babi and mother would lift it from under the dining room table, roll it up, and drag it down two flights of stairs, where they would hang it up on a line outside. Then with a willow rug beater they would take turns bashing it, watching the thick clouds of dust collect. Then upstairs again, where they'd rub it with watered-down ammonia before putting it back under the table. That's when my mother would notice the rug was a brilliant blue.

My mother remembers that when my babi did the laundry, her hands were chapped raw and red from the cold water.

My babi would place large, bulky linen or cotton sheets and duvet covers into an old wooden washing machine in the kitchen, which would wash things but never rinse. With the soap spilling out, my babi would drag the hulking wet bundles into the bathroom, put them into the bathtub and rinse the soap out. With her hands red and numb from cold and squeezing, she carried a tub from the second floor up the stairs to the sixth, to a dimly lit attic where she hung her laundry alongside the laundry of all the other residents in the building.

February 11, 2016

Dear Ben,

We are finishing our walk, the one that loops around Granville Island Market and runs along the ocean. You have been asking me to give you math equations to solve. You like numbers, how large some of them can get, how some seem to continue forever. You are on your scooter, one foot steady, the other pushing off the ground. You move fast, the way you do at most sports, at any activity really. Your energy seems infinite and you have little patience for things that don't move at warp speed. We climb the steps and you hook your scooter's handlebar over your shoulder.

"Mom, Babi was in the war, right?" you ask.

"Yes," I answer.

"Did she have weapons?"

"No," I say. "She was a prisoner. So was your great-grandfather, my děda."

"That's not fair," you say.

You swipe the fob to enter our building. When you take off your helmet, your curls are matted. I touch your hair and move it from your face. You are talking about practising drums and you start to negotiate how long you have to practise for. You have no idea, of course, of how your question has opened up inside me, wide, my body waiting, breathing, trepidatious.

That night you have nightmares.

Love always,
Mom

MY BABI WAS THE DECISION-MAKER in the family, a fearless leader, and also a lover of literature. She was a strong woman—a proponent of tough love. My děda called my babi "*domácí drak*," house dragon, because she was quick to anger. She would get mad at my mother frequently and sometimes chase her around the table with a wooden spoon. My děda would tell my babi to leave my mother alone. "*Lass sie*," he would say in German, thinking my mother couldn't understand.

My děda was gentle and when he spoke, his words were soft like clouds. My babi would call him a "*snilek*," a dreamer. He would sit by the window near the gramophone and listen to classical music. When he listened to the Czech composer, Antonín Dvořák, my děda would walk around the room and move his arms as if he were conducting an orchestra. In music and in nature, he always found beauty, and he often travelled to the Krkonoše Mountains with my mother.

Both my grandparents enjoyed talking politics, especially when they would learn about what was happening internationally, and out West. My grandparents found domestic politics boring due to the propaganda and fabrication of news from the Soviets. The West was portrayed as a dangerous enemy of the Soviet bloc countries who were joined to fight against this evil. My grandparents would sometimes get together with friends, also Holocaust survivors, and they would share jokes about Soviet and Czechoslovakian politicians.

Děda: "The news said Brehznev is in surgery."

Friend: "On his heart again?"

Děda: "No, he went to get his chest expanded to make room for another medal."

When they joked they kept their voices low. "The walls have ears," they would say.

LIFE UNDER THE COMMUNISTS was split into public and private spheres. My mother learned at a young age to be careful not to repeat anything at school about the politics she heard her parents discussing. Dissent wasn't tolerated. People would disappear and never be heard from again. My grandparents made the decision not to join the Communist Party, even though they wouldn't receive any promotions and my mother wouldn't be able to go to university. It was only the children whose parents were members of the Communist Party who were considered good students by the school.

Stores at that time hardly carried any merchandise and the clothing they did carry was ill-fitting and expensive. When my mother was young, my grandmother stayed home and bought a knitting machine and started her own business making sweaters. After that, my babi got a job in a carton-making factory. My děda worked as a buyer for the textile industry and he would travel to different towns and select fabric for manufacturers.

Sometimes my mother would receive hand-me-downs from relatives in Seattle, which she recalls were quite fashionable. When communism relaxed slightly in the late 1960s, jeans were allowed into the country, and kids lined up to buy them because they were excited to own something from the West. My mother remembers the jeans feeling like cardboard against her skin but she wore them anyway. One girl from my mother's class managed to smuggle a recording of The Beatles into school.

My mother was part of Pionýr, a socialist youth organization, and wore the requisite uniform of a red scarf, a white shirt and a blue skirt. Although membership in the group was voluntary, if my mother hadn't joined, a black mark would have been drawn against her and her family. On May 1, International Worker's Day, Pionýr members would march down Wenceslas Square waving Russian and Czechoslovak flags, shouting anti-West slogans.

There were lineups for everything from purchasing toilet paper to buying vegetables. Sometimes my mother would wait thirty minutes in line for her turn to go inside a store. There were shortages of everything. There was little meat to buy unless the butcher was friendly or there was extra money for a bribe. My mother remembers eating preserves in the winter along with apples, carrots, potatoes, cabbage, rye bread, jam and butter. For Sunday lunch, they enjoyed a small roast of pork with potatoes and caraway seeds.

When my mother was six, my děda sent her to get a jug of beer from the pub next door. They could buy milk, bread and cheese at the corner store. My mother would bring their metal milk canister and the woman at the store would use a ladle to fill it.

Doctors and dentists were bribed, often with food. My mother remembers Babi baking bread for the doctor. My mother had a root canal without anesthetic.

In the fall, my babi and děda ordered a pile of coal for their stove, which was stored in a cellar in the basement of the apartment building. When my děda would go down for coal, he would meet with his friend who also lived in the building, and they would discuss politics down there so as not to be overheard.

My děda would often listen to Radio Free Europe on his transistor radio. He kept the radio at low volume so the neighbours wouldn't hear and only listened in the living room, late into the night. Mostly he heard static, as the communists would jam the broadcast; nonetheless, he'd sit there with the radio pressed to his ear, trying to make sense of the jumble.

February 28, 2016

Dear Ben,

When your dad's grandfather passed away, you wrote a speech in his honour. You described what you remembered about your saba: visiting him at his house, going out for grilled cheese and French fries at a greasy spoon in Richmond, and playing with a big bouncy ball in the backyard.

Your grandpa and auntie stayed with us during this time, making our new apartment feel squished, but in a comfortable way, like a hug. I remember doing the same thing when my babi died. How you and I stayed with my parents for a week. In times of grief, sometimes being together in a tight huddle can offer support. In my family and in your dad's, it's not a normal thing to come together in this way. In this society, needing comfort, needing anything really, is a sign of weakness. I now know that this isn't true. Now I know that connection, that asking for help, the vulnerability, makes you stronger. When it happens, when we come together, it's special. And there is joy even in all the sorrow.

One evening your grandpa read aloud from a magazine produced by the Vancouver Holocaust Education Centre. You were nine years old as your grandpa began to recount the atrocities. I used my finger to slit my throat, and fortunately your grandpa understood and stopped reading immediately. Luckily you were oblivious. You just kept on reading your dragon novel, one leg thumping against the couch.

When do I let you know that one of your saba's jobs in the death camp was to wheel the dead bodies away? Or that your great-great grandfather killed himself in Theresienstadt? Or that your great-grandfather also took his life? How do I let you know about the murder of your ancestors? When is the right age to tell you the story of your family's genocide?

Love always,
Mom

WHEN MY MOTHER finished high school, my grandparents wanted her to improve her English language skills. My babi's cousin had a friend in England who needed an au pair. In June 1968, on the eve of her nineteenth birthday, my grandparents arranged for my mother to fly to London. The three of them were depressed when they arrived at the airport, as they had never been apart. "Don't talk to me or I will cry," said my mother.

She kissed my babi and my děda and pressed through the gate. My grandparents watched her board the giant Russian jet A62. It was the first time my mother had ever flown. I imagine her sitting in her seat looking out the small window. I imagine the fear gripping her chest as the plane sped down the runway. And as it lifted off into the blue sky, I imagine she felt the terror of being separated from her family.

When she landed, she went to work for a family with ten-year-old twin boys who had blazing red hair. My mother was amazed at how openly they lived as Jews. They didn't need to hide, and my mother learned about the culture and its traditions. But the family treated my mother poorly, as if she were a servant. In August, when the family with the twin boys went on vacation, another family who needed help was found and my mother switched and became the au pair for their three children.

My mother had every expectation of returning to Prague at the end of the summer. But her plans were disrupted on August 21, 1968, when Soviet and Warsaw Pact troops invaded Prague to end the reforms made by party leader Alexander Dubček during the Prague Spring. In a Jewish house in North London, my nineteen-year-old mother listened with her heart in her throat to the radio broadcast of the invasion. Her immediate impulse was to travel back home so she could fight for her country. The next day, with my grandparents' prompting, their cousins in Seattle, who had moved to the

United States before the war, sent my mother a telegram telling her to stay in London. They didn't want her to get stuck in a country under siege. As the panic set in, my mother wavered back and forth but finally agreed to stay.

It was my děda who made the decision to finally leave Prague.

"We didn't run when the Nazis came," he told my babi. "We didn't run when the communists took over in 1948. I'm not waiting around for the Russians to invade the rest of Europe."

On October 19, 1968, the borders were still open, so my babi flew to London to visit my mother. After they were reunited, my babi told my mother she had feared never seeing her again. The United States' refugee quota had already been filled but Canada had its doors open to Czechoslovakia. Together my babi and mother went to the Canadian Embassy, where they were interviewed. When the embassy officials asked my mother what she thought of communism, she told them it was a wonderful idea in theory but not the way it was being practised in the Soviet Union. My family received their immigration papers approving their status as refugees in Canada, and my babi flew back to Prague, where my grandparents applied for permission to leave on a "holiday" for two weeks in Vienna.

On November 25, 1968, at ten o'clock at night, my babi and děda crept down the granite stairs, out the sandy-coloured building where the doorway faced the backyard. They snuck to the front of the building. Instinctively, my babi looked up at their second-story apartment to check on the cat, even though they had already taken him to a friend's house in the country. The cat that sat at the window while the sheer curtains billowed in the wind. The cat that loved to climb up the curtains and dig his claws into them. The cat that fell out the window and managed only to bruise his chin.

The taxi stopped down the street. My babi saw an older woman look at the waiting car from a doorway, but she was too far away to identify who was leaving. My grandparents took five pieces of luggage instead of the original six they had packed so they wouldn't rouse the suspicion of authorities. At this point, the borders were still open but people were being questioned, some turned away and forced to return. For a second time, my děda wrote to his cousin in Seattle, he and my babi shut the door of their apartment with most of their belongings left behind: only this time, instead of being deported, they were leaving of their own free will.

My grandparents made it to the train station and boarded the train. They were still worried their luggage would draw attention and they wouldn't be allowed to cross the border. When the train stopped, a young man in uniform walked through the cabin to check passports. My grandparents told him they were going to Vienna on a two-week holiday. The man in uniform glanced at their passports.

"Have a nice trip," he said, and didn't even look at their luggage.

Even so, it still seemed like an eternity before the train started to move again. An hour later, when the train stopped for a second time, an Austrian customs official entered the cabin. He checked their documents and they were allowed to enter the country.

My grandparents were relieved once they crossed into Vienna. It was cold but sunny and they both felt they could at last breathe freely without being stopped and questioned. They went to Hotel Post and sent a telegram to their relatives in Seattle, who wired them money to pay for the hotel. Then my grandparents headed to the Canadian Embassy. They were still worried their plans would be thwarted, that the Canadian officials would change their minds, especially after examining my děda's x-ray, which showed traces of tuberculosis from the death camps. My babi and děda were older, fifty-seven and sixty-four respectively, and so my děda thought they might be considered a liability to their new country. But the officials accepted their reasons for leaving, that my grandparents didn't want to be separated from their only child, that they didn't want to keep living in constant fear as Jews, many now losing their jobs and being accused of being Zionists and enemies of the state aiming to overthrow the communist government.

My grandparents were hopeful when they were accepted as refugees and received aid. Officials arranged for their flight to Vancouver, and when my babi and děda left their passports at the Canadian Embassy, it was with a feeling of trust and ease, not with fear as it had been back at the Czech and Austrian borders.

On December 10, 1968, at eight o'clock in the morning, my grandparents took a taxi to the North station in Vienna. When they arrived, there were several groups already waiting, mostly young people, many with children. They spoke Czech or Slovak.

"It was an improved version of our deportation to Theresienstadt in 1942," my babi wrote in a letter to her cousin.

My grandparents boarded a bus to the airport in Schwechat, a town southeast of Vienna.

"I remember it was a clear day with no clouds, and the sun was beaming inside the plane as we travelled across what seemed like endless ocean," my babi wrote.

After twelve hours, they landed in Toronto and were given landed immigrant stamps in their passports.

In the meantime, on the same day, my mother had flown from London to Vancouver. She arrived before my grandparents, and when she saw them, her breath caught in her throat as she ran to greet them.

My mother recalls how overwhelmed she was by the beauty of the mountains, peaks dusted with snow, and as they drove over the Lions Gate Bridge—the iconic landmark that connects downtown Vancouver to West Vancouver—my mother was in tears. She knew she wouldn't return to Prague. She could feel it in her bones. If any of them had tried going back to Czechoslovakia, they would have been thrown in jail. This was her home now.

The family of three lived together in a motel on Capilano Road in North Vancouver, a low, sprawling beige building where the Canadian government had given them three free months of shelter. My mother remembers the motel being warm and cozy, with a living room, a bedroom and a kitchenette where my babi was able to cook. Since there were no lineups to buy meat, my babi made *řízky* (schnitzel) and potatoes, liver and tongue. In the room next door was another Czech refugee family with younger kids, and my mother found it comforting to have them close by.

My mother found a job at a bakery in West Vancouver. My děda was hired at a travel agency, working as a courier, delivering tickets. He bought a used Cortina, a garish purple, shaped like a hot rod. My babi worked as a house cleaner for a doctor. With this little income, my family was able to move into an apartment in West Vancouver, close to Park Royal, and slowly pay back the government.

When my děda had a heart attack, the doctor whose house Babi cleaned wrote to our relatives in Seattle, asking them for assistance in finding them a place to live. They agreed, and my babi found the apartment, which was purchased by her relatives. On February 14, 1972, they moved in. My grandparents paid for the maintenance fees, and once a year they would give our relatives a Canadian silver dollar, a symbolic gesture of gratitude.

Journal Entry #30

When I was in high school I made a charcoal drawing of a dying man, a rabbi with a big bushy beard, lying on the ground with a small broom in his hands, the words on the gate to Auschwitz, *Arbeit Macht Frei,* above his body. Although I knew subconsciously, I didn't fully understand the bitter irony of the words until I got much older. How the words—*work makes you free*—led to so many millions who would only find freedom through death.

Dear Ben,
Growing up, our family kept silent about the events from the past. My sister and I knew not to ask our babi questions about the Holocaust. This was not something our parents told us to do. It was something we inherently knew, much like my mother understood not to ask my babi and my děda questions about their past when she was growing up. We were all too scared to ask, to enter their trauma, to hurt them, to break them open. And so it stayed there, festering.

There's a silence in the stories I've never heard and never will. This silence wasn't quiet or still as you'd think. It was loud, took up space. Silence after the Holocaust turned to shame. Shame of surviving when others didn't. Survival guilt. Shame of being Jewish, of being treated as subhuman. Shame of nightmares and flashbacks. All this remained hidden under ugly beige broken-down communist blocks. Fear of persecution for a second time. Our family escaped—to Vancouver, with its ocean and mountains, its space, its freedom.

And yet.

Thirteen years after escaping from Czechoslovakia, and thirty-six years after liberation, my grandfather, my děda, would take his own life. He had been suffering from heart trouble and depression.

And yet.

Even here, surrounded by all this space, there remained a blanket, a thick cloud of silence. It sat between us as we played Scrabble, a heavy invisible force weighing down. No talking, only smoking. It was the early 80s. Sisters playing at Babi's. With our little hands, we rolled up the fresh crepes babi made for us and delicately and deliberately bit into them. As we unrolled the crepes, we showed each other our artwork, the beautiful snowflakes our mouths had carved out.

When I'm older and learn the truth, I can feel the silence of a window in my babi's bedroom. The silence of a widow. The shame of a suicide, hidden from children. The tension of bodies holding trauma. Of screams blistering under silence.

The beige wallpaper is textured. From a distance I think it looks glittery and woven; upon closer inspection, the edges are peeling. I pick at the place where the wallpaper curls. There is plaster underneath, exposed: a hint of black mold.

Love always,
Mom

My děda took his life when I was four. My mother was pregnant with my sister. At the time, I thought he died of old age or heart failure. I knew it wasn't cancer.

In old black and white photos, my děda looks mostly serious, but my mother says he was the soft one, kind and gentle. He wore a houndstooth cap and when he took it off, the top of his head was shiny and bald. He was quiet, introspective and pensive. He liked mountains and would often take trips to Krkonoše in the north to visit the high peaks and waterfalls. When he smiled there was sadness behind his eyes.

I don't remember my grandfather, my děda. I recognize him in the old photos, his smooth head, his cap, his rocking chair that would fall backwards when rocked too hard. My babi never sat in that rocking chair. Especially after he died. My sister and I would play with it, spin it around, make ourselves dizzy and sometimes fall over. With time, it became my father's chair. He would sit in it with a goofy grin, one leg crossed over his knee, navy shorts and brown sandals, black socks pulled to shins. And when my father's visits eventually became less frequent, it became my husband's.

I AM IN MY THIRTIES when my mother tells me my grandfather killed himself. I remember the casual nature of our conversation. How she is walking me from the kitchen to the bathroom and explaining his suicide along the way, as if she were describing the whereabouts of the extra toilet paper. When my mother tells me, I notice that I leave my body, a habit I formed when I was a girl. I can see my heart thump, see the tightening of muscles, feverish insides, cold extremities. It's called numbing out because I don't feel any of this. But I can see it happening as I stand outside my body, looking in.

As my mother talks, she tells me she understands why he did it, and we're standing in front of the bathroom and the door is open and I just want to go in there and close the door, but I can't because my mother is telling me that her father, my děda, was suffering. That he never fully recovered from the tuberculosis in the death camps, the haunting flashbacks, the heaviness of memory, the depression, the pain he carried.

That even though my mother had been three weeks shy of giving birth to my sister, my děda felt it necessary to end his life.

And so he jumped.

He jumped out of the bedroom window from the sixth floor of their apartment building. From the bedroom he shared with my grandmother. The bedroom my sister and I slept in when we stayed overnight. The bedroom we'd watch TV in. *The Muppet Show*, *Fraggle Rock*, *The Carol Burnett Show*, *The Golden Girls*.

The bedroom where my art hung on the wall: a lino print of hands, heart shaped open and offering an apple, beside the window where he jumped.

A FEW WEEKS AFTER my mother tells me about my děda's suicide, she says she's been thinking about how she could have done more. How she knew he was depressed. How she should have been watching him more closely. How she should have known something like this could happen. She says that at thirty-seven weeks pregnant, and with a three-and-a-half-year-old daughter, she wasn't paying much attention to the way my děda was feeling. That she wanted him to snap out of his depression, to be present, to see her, to witness her beautiful belly swelling, her daughter with her head of bouncing curls.

My děda was under the care of a psychiatrist and was taking Elavil, a drug often administered for depression. When I read the warnings about the drug on the Internet, there is a list that says people shouldn't take it if they've had a heart attack, which my děda did have back in 1971. I read about how in clinical studies Elavil caused suicidal thoughts. How there was an increased chance of becoming suicidal if taking this drug for depression.

Just before my grandfather jumped from the window, my mother noticed he was more quiet and downcast. There were dark circles under his eyes. He hadn't been sleeping well. He was still writing letters to Germany asking for compensation for the death camps, for everything they had lost during the Holocaust. He didn't get any reply.

There was only silence.

When my babi was walking home carrying bags of groceries, she noticed a crowd in front of their apartment building and an ambulance with its lights flashing. My babi knew before she got there that my děda was dead.

On May 30, 1981, one week after my děda turned seventy-seven, my babi called and spoke to my father. My mother was sitting on the couch in the living room. When he told my mother that her father had killed himself, she said it felt like a bolt from the sky. Her mind couldn't grasp it. She went numb. She couldn't understand how people outside kept on laughing, driving their cars, how the sun could still shine, that life could go on as it had before. She wanted the world to stop, to acknowledge her father, my děda, this man and his family, whose pain ran so deep.

In the mid-1990s, fifty years after the Holocaust, almost fifteen years after my děda had killed himself, and twenty years after he began writing to the Germans asking for compensation, my babi started receiving monthly pension from The Conference on Jewish Material Claims Against Germany. In 2003, at the age of ninety-two, sixty years after the Holocaust, twenty-two years after my děda committed suicide and eleven years before her death, my babi received compensation from the Endowment Fund for Victims of the Holocaust.

Journal Entry #33

I had a dream where my mother visits me in our old red character house except it isn't our old red character house, it's someone else's. There are large flat grey rocks lying on the ground. They look like tombstones, but they're not. My mother tells me she tried to commit suicide last year. She tells me this like it's no big deal. Like it's a shoulder shrug. Like everyone tries it at least once. She says she went outside and lay down on the ground and waited for the animals to eat her. But they didn't. And the fact that the animals didn't eat her is the only reason she's still alive.

WE USED TO VISIT my babi every Sunday. We'd visit for lunch and when she got older just for coffee and dessert. My babi sat at one end of the table, facing west to the ocean, her right side reflected off the window to the moody forest green of the North Shore mountains. Sometimes we'd play Scrabble and other times we'd just talk. She wanted to know how well we were doing in school, what we were writing about.

After we drank strong, black, drip coffee, we would move to the living room, my babi propped up on a few pillows, under a lamp, on the side closest to the kitchen. I would look over to see my babi's shiny brass collection, three full shelves collected over the years at flea markets and rummage sales. My favourites were little mice with tails sticking straight up, points sharp enough to take out an eye. My sister and I would spin on the chair, the one that belonged to my děda before he jumped. I looked out at the famous pink building outside the living room window, now so shabby chic, my eyes scanning beyond for the ocean.

My mother never told anyone about my děda's suicide because my babi didn't want people to know. That my děda took his own life carried a shame so thick that my family told everyone he had died of a heart attack at home.

There was no funeral, no celebration of life, no *shiva* for my děda. And three weeks after he died, my mother gave birth to my sister.

Journal Entry #36

I learn that depression and PTSD in survivors of the Holocaust is common. How Holocaust survivors are three times more likely to commit suicide due to unresolved trauma and depression. How trauma and chronic stress lead to an increase in suicide and attempted suicide among elderly survivors. These survivors are often struggling with feelings of hopelessness, depression, unresolved grief and preoccupation with the dead. That severely depressed survivors, like my děda, are at high risk for attempted suicide.

I Google Primo Levi after I read his book, *Survival in Auschwitz*, for the second time. Wikipedia tells me he died from injuries after falling from a third-floor apartment landing. Some people don't believe it was a fall. He was sixty-seven.

IN THE CONCENTRATION CAMPS, approximately one out of four people committed suicide. My mother tells me that Bedřich, my great-grandfather, my děda's father, killed himself in Theresienstadt in 1943.

My mother doesn't tell me how he did it. She doesn't know.

She does tell me how Bedřich suffered from depression after Hitler invaded Prague. A sign was taped to his grocery store's window that read *Jüdisches Geschäft, Jewish Shop.* How he was forcibly removed from his home just outside of Prague, in a town called Blatná, and imprisoned.

Just before my děda jumped out the window, just before he took his own life, did he think of his father?

Journal Entry #39

I send my mother an email about a question I have and when I type Děda's name, my phone autocorrects and spells the word *dead*.

Book Two

"To grow up with overwhelming inherited memories, to be dominated by narratives that preceded one's birth or one's consciousness, is to risk having one's own life stories displaced, even evacuated, by our ancestors. It is to be shaped, however indirectly, by traumatic fragments of events that still defy narrative reconstruction and exceed comprehension. These events happened in the past, but their effects continue into the present."

—Marianne Hirsch
The Generation of Postmemory:
Writing and Visual Culture after the Holocaust
Columbia University Press, 2012

"Even if the person who suffered the original trauma has died, even if his or her story lies submerged in years of silence, fragments of life experience, memory, and body sensations can live on, as if reaching out from the past to find resolution in the minds and bodies of those living in the present."

—Mark Wolynn
It Didn't Start With You: How Inherited Family Trauma
Shapes Who We Are and How to End the Cycle
Viking, 2016

March 5, 2016

Dear Ben,

In biblical Hebrew, Benjamin means *son of the right hand*. In the Hebrew Bible, Benjamin was the youngest son of Jacob and the ancestor of one of the twelve tribes of Israel. In a more spiritual sense, scholars have interpreted Ben to mean *build* or *rebuild*.

Ben, you are the son of our family, the great-grandson of Holocaust survivors. You are named after Ben Zion, your father's favourite uncle, also a survivor of the Holocaust.

You survived your birth and together we are a family. Rebuilding. We are slowly gathering the pieces and building a life, creating a narrative.

Your story is one of rebirth.

Love always,
Mom

IT WASN'T THAT I WAS OBSESSED with having a baby. Deciding to have a child was the next logical step in our relationship. Jeremy and I had a place to live, we both had full-time jobs, we had a dog. I was twenty-eight and my eggs weren't getting any younger. It's not like everyone was doing it. But it was something we both wanted to try, at least once. Plus, I was kind of bored. There hadn't been any grand epiphany or giant Zeus-like thunderbolt. It was a simple conversation Jeremy and I had together, just as if we had been choosing what kind of cheese to get at the deli: Cheddar or Swiss?

I never really liked other people's kids, unless they were children of good friends. I had jobs teaching kids or playing with them, but at the end of the day I could give them back. I found those jobs draining and it led me to feel some compassion toward my own father, who was a grade seven math and science teacher for thirty years.

When my period was late the next month, I peed on a stick. As we watched the line darken on the test, we were both surprised and so I did another just to make sure. I held it up, my hands shaking. I didn't know whether to jump up and down or cry. I panicked. We weren't ready. I immediately began to miss my old life before child.

What had we done?

I became what they refer to in medical terms as a *fertilized* woman. As the blastocyst grew, I bought books and read websites and kept up with the development unfolding in my uterus. My breasts grew heavier, my stomach rolls multiplied and I couldn't get off the couch without wanting to vomit. At the same time, I was so hungry. Voraciously so. I ate cheeseburgers and pickles and potato chips. I devoured large, drippy cinnamon buns slathered with cream cheese icing. I went on a pill to curb my nausea so I could get off the couch and go to work. Leah referred to my fetus as "Buddy" and my mother called it "The Parasite." Jeremy and I agreed not to find out the sex even though he really wanted to know.

I hadn't spent a lot of time around babies before and had only changed one poopy diaper when I babysat at the age of fifteen. And even then I panicked, calling the infant's grandmother because she was on speed-dial and I had forgotten the how-to-put-on-a-diaper instructions from my grade seven babysitting course.

I still got shit on one of my hands.

I'M CONVINCED ultrasounds are a form of torture, invented by the same kind of men who must have been the ones who came up with other medieval instruments designed to oppress women, such as bras, high heels, nylons and bathing suits. And if drinking six glasses of water two hours before an ultrasound and then asking a pregnant woman to hold her pee in doesn't sound like torture to you, then good for you—you are stronger than I am.

Because all I wanted to do was pee. I wanted to break the dam and release the flood, but instead I clenched and my legs shook and I performed a seated pee dance. In the chair next to mine, one of Jeremy's knees bounced up and down in solidarity. He put a hand on my thigh and sighed, ran his other hand through his hair.

When I couldn't stand it anymore, I shuffled to the front desk, making sure they could see the desperation on my face, the sweat on my brow.

"You may go to the bathroom and release a small amount of urine," was what one uniformed woman said.

I felt my eye twitch as I backed away from the counter and looked at the bathroom, its door open a crack, large enough for me to witness the beauty of the white porcelain bowl. I decided to try, even though I had only done my kegels that one time in that one prenatal yoga class I took out of guilt for not exercising enough.

I squatted over the toilet because I don't like to sit on public seats, making sure my thighs and feet were firmly planted, and let go. It had to be the least satisfying pee of my life. My stream wouldn't stop. Finally I managed to tame the flow down to a dribble, which kept dribbling. I hiked up my underwear, now wet with leaking urine, and pulled up my pants. When I walked out of the bathroom, it was like nothing had spilled out of me. The dam was ready to burst again.

When we were finally called into a room and I sat down, I thought I would pee all over the table. But I held it together even though it was still winter and the room was freezing and I thought I could see my breath. Even when the technician squirted cold gel all over my belly. Even when she pressed the probe straight into my bladder and I thought I would explode.

At the end of the ultrasound, all we got was a crappy picture of our alien-like baby, his hand strategically placed in front of his face, as if he had put it there on purpose, just to say: "No pictures please."

MY SISTER-IN-LAW had two of her kids at home and my first mom friend had three successful home births. The idea of giving birth in the strange, sterile environment of a hospital—with its long list of rules, its bright fluorescent lighting and pukey green curtains—wasn't appealing. We lived in the Wild West, majestic mountains, magnificent ocean, home to doulas and midwives and pot smokers. There weren't rules here.

We were equipped with extra sheets and waterproof underpads. We had towels, receiving blankets, washcloths and garbage bags. I froze maxi-pads so I could use them for my throbbing crotch post-birth and a sitz bath kit in case of tearing. I wasn't just prepared, I was over-prepared. I made lists, I had numbers. Midwives, doula, doctor, St. Paul's Hospital. I had a birth plan. And that plan was to stay home. Despite worry from family and friends, I didn't have any expectations we'd see the inside of a hospital. I didn't absorb their comments. In my mind, our baby was going to come out into the safe quiet of our bedroom.

March 8, 2016

Dear Ben,

My midwife appointments became a chore after awhile, especially toward the last trimester. The whooshing of your heart
with the Doppler, the urine testing, the blood pressure check,
the stepping on the scale, the *see you next visit*. I grew concerned that I was too detached, that I wasn't bonding with
you properly, that I wasn't talking to you enough, wasn't playing as much Mozart as I should. But really, I had no idea what
or who was growing inside me—no clue what to expect.

I did know that my body wasn't mine anymore.

Love always,
Mom

WHEN I WAS FIVE MONTHS PREGNANT, Jeremy and I travelled to New York. We hadn't been there before and decided to visit before we were strapped down with the weight of a baby. I remember eating hot dogs from most of the street vendors on most of the corners within a ten-block radius of our hotel. Central Park, Times Square, Broadway shows, fried chicken and grits with a family friend, a visit with another, walking, walking, always walking, a river cruise, Statue of Liberty, art and museums, concrete jungle.

And then, one afternoon, my breasts sprang a leak. I'm not talking about a faucet of water. It came out more in dribbles. At first I thought I might be dying. Clear fluid slowly oozing out of my nipples. It still makes me squeamish when I think about it. I have to stop and hold onto my breasts as I write this. Jeremy was completely useless. He just sat there and grinned. This being his traditional response for when my breasts decide to make an appearance. So I cracked open the laptop and Googled "leaky breasts." Turns out it wasn't my time to leave earth yet. Google came up with pages of information telling me it was just colostrum or what they call pre-milk. Still it was quite unsettling at five months pregnant. I wasn't ready for things to spill out of my body yet. I still had four months left.

WHEN MY MOTHER WAS SIX MONTHS PREGNANT with me, she missed the bus that would have taken her an hour away to the university library where she worked in cataloguing. She ran as fast as her body would allow, one hand forming a cradle under her belly. But the driver didn't wait for her. The bus drove away, leaving my mother in a cloud of exhaust.

My mother dropped her purse and her backpack on the ground and leaned against the bus stop. She took big gulps of air while she waited for her insides to finish swirling. It probably felt as though someone was trying to rip her stomach apart. She might have thought she was going to give birth right there on the frozen February sidewalk.

The next day, my mother went out and bought a used red Datsun. She didn't take the bus to work again. After she had me, she quit.

March 23, 2016

Dear Ben,

In my belly you hiccupped all the time. The midwives said it was a good thing, that you were strengthening your heart muscles and learning how to breathe. You moved and kicked and turned, especially whenever I began to fall asleep.

Your grandma would tell me stories about your dad, the way he would kick her so hard she could see the outline of his feet as he pushed against her skin. She said he'd do so many somersaults that her blouse would shake and people would stare at her belly. Her doctor and friends told her not to worry about your dad's activity. That babies were different once they were born.

Before he was six months old, your dad pulled himself out of his crib and rolled into the hallway closet. When your grandma went to check on him, she thought he had been kidnapped.

Love always,
Mom

IN MY THIRD TRIMESTER I picked up a book called *Birthing from Within: An Extra-Ordinary Guide to Childbirth Preparation.* I forced myself to read it even though I was resistant. It was for people, like myself, who wanted to experience birth *au naturel,* but as I read it, it didn't feel like it was written for me. It was written for that other woman, the one with the long, golden locks, the flowing clothes, commune-style living, glass bottles only, organic everything, breastfeeding and no supplementing with formula, the journal-writing, scrapbooking, judgey mother who I feared. Plus the book had exercises.

One day when we were away at a cabin, in a moment of weakness, I decided to do an exercise. I can't remember what it said exactly, but I do remember it had something to do with holding an ice cube as a way of practising for what labour might feel like. So I sat there in an Adirondack chair in the middle of the lawn in my black sundress, my belly swelling its third-trimester swell, and tried to hold an ice cube in my hand.

I tried.

I really did.

But it burned.

It felt like the ice was carving a hole into the flesh of my palm. So I threw the cube as hard as I could and wiped my palm on my dress and cuddled my frozen hand until it felt warm and ready and alive enough to try again. I must have made a dozen attempts, and with each failure, I felt more deflated.

How was I going to push a human out of my vagina if I couldn't hold onto a fucking ice cube?

I was already failing before I had even begun.

MY MOTHER TELLS ME I was born on one of the hottest August days on record. She started having contractions around five o'clock in the morning. When the pain didn't dissipate, she woke my father and they drove to the Vancouver General Hospital. There, the nurse examined my mother and she was eventually sent to a birthing room. My mother remembers how the window in her room was smeared with dirt and fingerprints, and how wasps were buzzing around it. She remembers the laughing gas, how it made her feel like she was floating near the ceiling, but didn't make her laugh. My mother remembers the reclining bed, how my father and the nurse helped her sit so she could push, how when the doctor came she pushed a few more times until I was born around eleven in the morning.

THE SEX OF OUR BABY was pretty much 100 percent confirmed by a crazy old Russian woman. We were having a yard sale to get rid of old junk before we had to buy new junk for the baby. She hobbled up to me, put her hands on my belly and said, "You're having a boy."

Although I didn't grow up with brothers, I had many boys as friends and we'd play for hours with Transformers, He-Man and Lego. We'd invent elaborate games with wrestling moves that involved placing sleeping bags over our heads and swinging baseball bats at each other. Boys were simple, out there and fun.

And yet I didn't know a thing about them.

How their bodies worked, their erections, their wet dreams, their cracking voices in puberty. The way they jostled each other in the school hallways or put each other in headlocks. The fact that males don't live as long as females, that they are more likely to die by suicide.

And so when the crazy Russian lady touched my belly and gave me the prophecy, I was in awe of the little mystery growing inside my uterus. How was I going to raise one when they were all so peculiar?

THE DAY BEFORE my mother was born, my babi and my děda walked ten kilometres across Prague to visit a cousin. On the walk back home, my babi started having contractions. So they boarded a tram and went to the hospital. My mother doesn't remember my babi telling her about the birth, only that she was born quickly and early the next morning.

My babi couldn't breastfeed.

She had no milk.

WHEN MY MIDWIVES TOLD ME I was going to be late, I got angry. My back was hurting, I was exhausted, my legs were swollen, it was the hottest summer on record, I had to pee every five minutes and I had abdominal separation that caused burning on the top of my stomach.

After I left the appointment, I shuffled slowly up the street and went to a café where I ate the biggest cinnamon knot I'd ever seen and then went home and stuck my feet in the purple elephant pool Jeremy had purchased to cool off my swollen ankles.

My baby was healthy and comfortable. Too comfortable. So comfortable he didn't want to budge. I've heard this about boys. How they just want to stay in the warm, soft place of their mothers and never come out.

Journal Entry #41

Sometimes I hear the sound of ambulance sirens when there are no emergency vehicles around. It happens mostly when I'm driving, but especially when I'm driving alone.

Dear Ben,

On September 17, 2006, the morning I awoke to contractions, Jeremy and I went to the Vancouver Baby & Family Fair. I had intended to write about the baby product industry even though I was reluctant to go because of the crowds. We slowly waded through the booths and throngs of people. At the last booth, standing next to a silver statue of Buddha, was a large, bald-headed man with a snake. He called me over and wrapped a thick green-and-yellow boa constrictor around my shoulders. He told me of an ancient story from Thailand and said if I rubbed the snake, I would have an easy labour. On September 17, almost sixteen years ago, your dad and I went on our first date. It's also my lucky number. So I rubbed the snake.

That night, as my contractions grew stronger, we ate spaghetti and meatballs, which I later barfed up, and it reminded me of the time when I was little and had the stomach flu and managed to puke up my noodles still whole.

As the labour progressed, I howled like an animal and later found out I had woken our neighbour's teenage son, two houses down, by repeatedly screaming "Jesus, O Lord," so loudly he had to get up and move to the basement. The doula told me I was having back labour due to your preference for holding a posterior position. Already you were looking to make a statement, as if you were saying, "Hello beautiful world, I want to enter you face up with my eyes open."

I remember drinking Gatorade and crunching on multicoloured Life Savers. I remember washcloths on my forehead and sips of water. Somehow my clothes came off and I remained naked until you were born.

Labour is a fascinating thing.

My body wasn't my own. Something took over. It was primal, pure and raw. A deep growling from within. Everything went fuzzy but at the same time everything was perfectly clear. I knew what I had to do. In the early stages, before the pushing started, it was perhaps the only time I can say I truly inhabited my body.

By early morning I was ten centimetres dilated and ready to push, although the urge for me to do so wasn't there. My two midwives were a little perplexed, as this feeling usually comes naturally toward the end of labour, so they told me to push anyway. Jeremy was by my side and I used him to lean on, and at one point I think he was pushing harder than I was.

After the first hour of pushing, I was exhausted. At the end of three hours, I was panicked because I had read that if things took this long I should be going to the hospital. The midwives weren't worried. They told me that we could go to the hospital but that it was normal to push for several hours with a first baby. At this point we were catching a glimpse of the top of your beautiful head, your mass of dark brown hair. Besides, they said, if we left now, I would probably give birth in the ambulance. My instinct told me to go to the hospital. But I ignored it and continued to push. After four hours, I pushed so hard the IV popped out of my arm.

Then your heart rate dropped.

Love always,
Mom

April 7, 2016

Dear Ben,

I knew we were in trouble when the midwives disappeared downstairs. When they came back up we heard them whispering. The urge to push hit me hard then, but the midwives warned me not to because every time I did, your heart rate dropped. Not being able to push during contractions was probably the most physically challenging thing I've ever done. I was going against the natural birthing process. I clung to my doula's hand and breathed. I heard the murmuring voices of Jeremy and the midwives. We learned you were in distress. An ambulance was called. I went numb.

What happened next unfolded like a flipbook, fast and slow at the same time. I had a circle of burly firemen hovering over my nearly naked body (your dad had outfitted me with my small bathrobe that draped open because of my big belly), busying themselves with strapping me to a chair and carrying me down three flights of stairs in an upright position. The midwives were hovering, the ambulance attendants were running, and there I was at ten in the morning, pulled out of my house into late-summer sunshine, where a group of concerned and bug-eyed neighbours stood watching the chaos.

Into the ambulance we went, your dad sitting up front and one of my midwives holding an oxygen mask over my face, helping me breathe through the contractions. I sucked on that oxygen as hard as I could. My world was spinning, my body and mind flooded with shock as pain and panic ripped through me.

At the hospital I left my body. I floated up to the ceiling and watched the frantic movements of the medical staff, the blinding bright lights. A nurse yelled at me for making too much noise. "Stop screaming!" she ordered. They gave me a spinal, or maybe they didn't—I don't remember. They asked if we wanted forceps or a C-section, but then they said, "Forget it, there's no time." It was an emergency and they needed to get you out right away, so they put me under and everything went black.

Love always,
Mom

April 16, 2016

Dear Ben,
At five minutes after noon, your first breath was a non-breath. The inhale didn't come.

Asphyxia.

Baby limp and apneic with meconium present.

Your dad watched as the doctors scrambled with a mask to put on you, a quiet purple baby. It was a silent horror unfolding.

IPPV carried out for two minutes with heart rate of more than 100 throughout.

Two minutes: first gasp of regular breathing.

Me, lying strapped to a table, unconscious, general anesthetic, dreamless and ignorant to the terror. I feel fortunate for this unconsciousness. In my mind, the memory would have replayed a million times over, like a busy signal. Like the ancestral memories I hold in my body.

I might have lost it. I might have gone insane.

Your dad watched everything through a tiny window in the door. When breath finally found you, it then stopped again, and you were rushed out of the room.

CPAP maintained until seven minutes, baby cried and moved spontaneously.

Respiratory distress. Mild decrease in tone.

I was wheeled away in the opposite direction to be sewn up.

No seizures.

Cord prolapse, AKI, hyponatremia, severe acidosis, transient renal dysfunction.

Acute kidney injury.

Urine positive for blood.

Antibiotics for forty-eight hours.

Your dad was left standing in the middle of the hallway, not knowing where to go. So he called his father in Calgary and his father drove to the airport and jumped on the next plane to Vancouver.

Paging nephrology.
Paging neurology.

Love always,
Mom

April 22, 2016

Dear Ben,

While my eyes were still shut, I saw white light and heard voices. It felt like I was swimming from somewhere deep and it was taking a long time to surface. When I opened my eyes, your dad was leaning over smiling at me. He wheeled me down on my stretcher, flat on my back, to see you for the first time.

You were so beautiful. Tiny, pale, a wrinkled baby with a wild patch of dark brown hair. My crumpled and worn incubator baby with tubes and pins and needles. When I reached in to touch you, your little fingers wrapped around mine. Even at a few hours old, your grip was strong and I knew then I was dealing with a fighter.

A survivor.

Love always,
Mom

May 3, 2016

Dear Ben,

I was grateful for the drips of morphine and the catheter because it meant I didn't have to get up, didn't have to *feel* anything.

My obstetrician came to me in a dream, an angel with a blond bob and glasses, who peered at my incision and declared how excellent it looked. I received many compliments on that cut. "What a tidy job," doctors would say. "What a neat little scar. Hardly noticeable."

Your dad slept on a tiny mattress on the floor next to me. We listened to Billy Joel because that's all we had on the laptop. But I wouldn't have changed the music. It was perfect and simple. When "Piano Man" came on, I could sing along. "He says, 'Bill, I believe this is killing me,' as the smile ran away from his face. 'Well I'm sure that I could be a movie star if I could get out of this place.' Oh, la, la la, di da da, La la, di da da da dum."

I sat on the bed in my toothpaste-blue hospital gown, icing my engorged breasts, which were large as boulders. "You've got enough milk to feed all the babies in this hospital," a doctor joked.

I pumped.

I pumped my colostrum, and my fresh breast milk squirted through a rubber tube into small vials, which I poured carefully to the 60mL mark, labelled with *Ben Sicherman* and stuck in a bar fridge. I pumped alongside women whose babies were next to mine in the Neonatal Intensive Care Unit (NICU), babies who were smaller than my fist, babies who might or might not be able to breathe air outside the hospital walls.

It's a different world inside a hospital. Time stops, or moves agonizingly slow. The outside—the sky—seems so far away, distant, unreachable.

I looked out a window once and caught sight of the clouds and I prayed. Or rather, I pleaded. I wasn't sure to whom I was praying, but an image of our dog, who had died the week before, appeared in the clouds and so I prayed to her. She came with her big, drooling Newfoundlander head and mangled back legs and so I prayed to her to please keep you alive.

Love always,
Mom

May 6, 2016

Dear Ben,

The umbilical cord, the string that connects you to me, was compressed and wrapped around your neck three times. With each push, your heart rate decelerated. The doctors didn't know how you had survived that long without oxygen.

Your kidneys shut down. The kidneys, we were told, are the first organs to stop working when the brain doesn't receive enough oxygen.

One night I woke up and lost it. I cried and cried. I was so scared. Your dad got up onto my small hospital bed and just held me.

Love always,
Mom

May 19, 2016

Dear Ben,
When you were born I couldn't feed you right away. For the first two days and part of the third, you were hooked up to an IV. You had a catheter to monitor your urine output. Your rolling veins, the pricks in your toes. The doctors were checking your kidneys. You weren't peeing and your sodium levels were very low.

On the third day you peed on one of the nurses when she tried to insert the catheter. A good sign. They gave you the nickname "Gentle Giant" because at six pounds you were the largest baby in the NICU.

When the midwives came for a visit, they said that in all their years of practising midwifery, they had never had an experience quite like your birth. We were quiet after they told us this. We didn't know how to respond.

I was able to breastfeed when you were three days old. One of the midwives showed me how to move your head to my breast. It felt as though I was slamming your head against my nipple, but it worked and you started to nurse right away. I called you my baby wombat because of your wrinkles and I listened to your little snorting noises as I rocked you in the chair.

I have no words for what it felt like to hold you for the first time.

Love always,
Mom

June 1, 2016

Dear Ben,

On day five I became unhinged. The skies were gloomy, foreboding and pissing rain. Your brain required testing. First you had a CAT scan. They strapped you down and you screamed until you were the colour of a beet. Then the worst moment. We had to sign a waiver before doing the MRI. The waiver said that if you didn't wake up after going under general anesthetic, the hospital was not at fault.

When my pen touched the paper, I felt as if I were signing your life away. I was so scared you wouldn't wake up. I cried and waited. Waited and cried.

Then the doctor called us into a small room. We huddled in with the rest of our family. My parents, my in-laws, my sister. The doctor said that babies have these incredible, adaptable brains. The fact that you were healthy and your brain showed no signs of injury was, according to the doctor, dumbfounding.

"Your baby is a miracle," she said.

I threw myself at your dad, and we held each other, our bodies shaking. After some hugs our family left us to sit quietly. You are a miracle, I thought. I felt the love in and around us. My father-in-law brought us burgers and fries so we wouldn't have to eat more mushy peas and Jell-O. He sat on the hospital floor, telling stories while we ate. A good friend brought me my favourite dark chocolate. Another brought a bouquet with September's yellow sunflowers.

There is no rational explanation for why you entered the world the way you did, or how you survived, but I can say for sure that you were never alone.

Love always,
Mom

June 12, 2016

Dear Ben,

On the sixth day, the sun split through the shadowy mass. When they told us we could take you home, it felt as if we were floating in a dream. We strapped you in your car seat and your head fell horizontal and we were worried your neck would break off so I cupped your head with my hand while your dad carried you. We walked outside like zombies, all squinty-eyed and foggy. We were so glad to be leaving the hospital but at the same time we were nervous to go. What if something happened? What if there was another emergency? What if you stopped breathing?

Your dad and I stood on the hospital sidewalk, you in your car seat in the hook of his elbow. Your grandpa pulled up in his rental car. The sun reflecting off the car window hurt my eyes. Your dad adjusted your car seat inside, while I stood there, my feet glued to the cement.

We got into the car and rolled down our windows. We took deep breaths of air, felt the cool early fall wind on our faces. The hint of yellow, orange and red on leaves of old maple trees lining the streets. People walking dogs, drinking coffee, reading newspapers. Kids playing on a jungle gym at an elementary school. It felt as if the earth was offering us an invitation to a fresh new day, full of life.

Love always,
Mom

BOOK THREE

"It isn't easy to be happy if you're a Jew. As you float along on your happiness, the fingertips of the six million brush you from beneath, like kelp reaching up from the bottom of the sea."
—Kim Masters
Daughters of Absence: Transforming a Legacy of Loss
Dream of Things, 2012

"Thus, trauma is transmitted intergenerationally, and can be observed through various life patterns, including dietary, relational, and religious decisions; a general attitude towards the world marked by excessive guilt, fear and the expectation of death; and a devotion of one's life to an ever-present, unspoken story that must be reconstructed like pieces of a puzzle. That is, amidst debilitating silences and deeply rooted family secrets, third generation Holocaust survivors attempt to construct the foundation of a narrative for their predecessors, and indirectly for themselves."
—Nirit Gradwohl Pisano
Granddaughters of the Holocaust:
Never Forgetting What They Didn't Experience
Academic Studies Press, 2012

June 27, 2016

Dear Ben,

When you laugh so hard you can't breathe, you get the hiccups. We stop wrestling for a moment and allow breath to enter your lungs. I don't know why you still hiccup when you laugh. Remember how I've told you about how you once hiccupped in my womb too? Deep belly shaking ones. How the hiccups were helping prepare your lungs for breath by contracting your diaphragm?

And yet when you were born you had no breath.

Born still. Quiet. Limp.

Now you're loud. You're out there. You're nine. You don't stop moving.

But the hiccups are still there.

They're a reminder for me. A trigger. A flashback.

And you throw yourself on me, your head of brown mushroom curls, and we nuzzle the nuzzles of mother and son.

And this love feels like wanting to kill someone and wanting them to never leave your side.

And I inhale deep and feel my heart ready to burst because life does not get more tender than this moment of loving and fearing and heaving in this place that sounds as large as symphonies and as quiet as the flutter of butterfly wings.

Love always,
Mom

WHEN I AM TIRED, I sleep heavy and black. But those nights are rare. I usually don't remember my dreams and I awaken at least once, maybe twice. I am up with the first hint of sunlight and asleep with the first wave of night. My sleep is halting, afraid.

I am sitting in a free workshop on how to heal trauma. The panel tells us they can cure us with a combination of hypnotherapy, massage and counselling. That trauma can be used as a vehicle for transformation and doesn't have to be a prison.

They select a woman from the audience who has raised her hand to volunteer. She is young and energetic, with short brown hair and swirling earrings. The hypnotherapist and the massage guy each do their thing and the woman is moved to a different realm and they rub her shoulders and talk smooth words in her ears and it is fast, like a dance, and I soon tire of listening. The woman has her eyes closed; they tell us she's asleep, but she speaks the entire time and with a snap of the fingers she's awake and feels great and so wonderful and what a life-changing experience that was.

I am skeptical.

"What about working with intergenerational trauma?" I ask the panel during question period.

"Yes, I do that," responds the hypnotherapist, and he talks about how he works with past lives.

I wait impatiently, my blood simmering like hot soup.

"I meant in this current life," I say.

He doesn't get it and speaks again about past lives and my heart sinks and I try to breathe but feel the burn of tears instead.

I watch the woman next to me tear a page out of her notebook. She writes a name on it and a word that I can't decipher from the angle I'm at. But somehow I know she is writing it for me.

The question period ends and I find the workshop is more of a sales pitch than anything. Six sessions for a thousand dollars and a promise that the trauma will vanish. The hypno-therapist snaps his fingers. It's a tempting offer and a lineup forms by the cash register.

The woman turns to me. I can feel her sadness in her quiet. She has hair like mine, a big frizzy mess of curls.

"Epigenetics," she says. "Does that word sound familiar?"

I shake my head no.

"This is a name of a healer, a shaman, who does ancestral healing. Give her a call. I've been working with her."

She hands me the piece of paper.

"Let me guess. Grandparents were also Holocaust survivors?" she asks.

I suck in air and my stomach tightens. I nod.

"Hyper-vigilance," she says. "Do those words mean anything?"

My skin prickles with recognition. My heart is beating a thousand times per second. So fast it might explode.

"I haven't heard that term before," I answer. "I usually tell people it's as though I'm perched on top of a watchtower on the lookout for sabre-toothed tigers. I'm vigilant, alert, eyes scanning for danger. I don't have any relief. There are no reserves. I am it—I am all there is. I don't have an off button. If I'm not always watching, if my body and mind are not always in fight or flight, and my cortisol turned on overdrive, some-thing terrible could happen. My son is exactly the same way."

"Yes, that's it," she says. "My kids are also riddled with anxiety. When my daughter was four she was attacked by a pit bull." She rolls up the sleeve of her shirt. I see two large red circles that look like puncture wounds. "I intervened," she says.

I stare at her scars and then her eyes meet mine and she quickly rolls down her shirt.

"I have to go," she says. "Good luck."

I touch her leg and thank her.

She gathers her things and flies out the door before I can ask her name.

Journal Entry #44

Holocaust survivors are getting older and many have since passed. What will we do when there are none left? Who will carry their voices? How will we ensure that we remember? That we don't stay silent? That we awaken to the atrocities we are now committing and to the ones we are capable of committing?

July 2, 2016

Dear Ben,

I watch *Nova: The Ghost in Your Genes*, a program on epigenetics where researchers tell me that the lives of our parents, grandparents and great-grandparents can directly affect us even though we may not have experienced the events ourselves. I read about the transgenerational transmission of trauma, about the fact that genes can be altered and carry memories of experiences, which are then passed down. We, the next generations, hold these changes, these memories, in our bodies.

I learn that children of Holocaust survivors show abnormal levels of stress hormones, which means coping with stress is difficult and they are more prone to PTSD. Because the gene that manages the stress response has been damaged, it's as if their bodies are in a constant state of hyper-arousal.

This genetic imprint is then passed onto their children.

The grandchildren.

The third generation.

Which means trauma gets inherited. Which means me. Jeremy.

Generation four: I'm afraid for what you may carry in you.

Love always,
Mom

Journal Entry #49

I watch my mother as she finishes an apple. She doesn't eat it like a typical North American mother. She tears into it like it's the best thing she's ever tasted. She devours the entire thing. Her teeth bite through skin, to the flesh, and when she's done that, she finishes the core. She even swallows the seeds. When I was young I used to worry she would die from cyanide poisoning from always eating those seeds.

I carry snacks with me wherever I go. I avoid ever feeling hungry. Hunger scares me. I grow shaky and unstable. There is fear in not having enough, of running out, of not knowing when the next meal will be.

I come from a family that knows starvation. Whose bellies weren't distended from eating too much, but whose bodies were so deprived, I imagine it felt like a bunch of knives were cutting up their insides.

My family never throws out food. Leftovers become second and third leftovers. Furry bits of mold lovingly and carefully scraped off.

Now I use my compost. But only when my mother isn't looking.

I AM SUPER ORGANIZED and chronically over-prepared (it's not OCD, I checked). Yes, *I am* that person. Need a Band-Aid? I have one. Need a tiny one for the little toe? I have one of those too. Hungry? Here, have a granola bar. Not satisfied? Have some beef jerky. Thirsty? Here's some water. Need a pen? Got it. What about some paper? An extra bag to carry stuff? Check. Hand sanitizer, tampons, water, Kleenex, painkillers, two different kinds of mints, bobby pins, hair elastics, Chap Stick. The list goes on. I am, to put it simply, always prepared. When disaster strikes, I'm the person. (If over-preparedness isn't in the DSM, it should be.)

When Ben was a baby, I'd stroll around Vancouver with the biggest diaper bag in the city. Actually, it wasn't really a diaper bag. It was a giant duffel bag that I turned into a diaper bag. It weighed so much it used to tip the stroller over when he wasn't in it.

I had to be prepared. Shit happens. Especially with babies. Literally. Shit up Ben's back, to the folds in his neck, out the sides, down the legs. I had every kind of wipe available on the market in 2006, a change of clothes for the baby, a change of clothes for me, toys, books, snacks, changing pads, Ziplocs (for poopy diapers), blankets, hats, rain suit, mittens.

In September 2000, when I took my first tentative steps into Jeremy's apartment, I saw a giant fridge magnet that said: *Cheer up, the worst is yet to come.* I think it was that magnet that helped seal our relationship.

I've decided to blame this hyper-vigilance and over-preparedness on intergenerational trauma. Where else do we Jews get our neuroses, which have been documented and stereotyped for years? "Jewish women are in their heads too much," is a comment I often hear when I'm obsessing about something for the hundredth time. My own mother used to tell me, "Don't sweat the small stuff," and "Just go with the flow." But I'm not a go-with-the-flow type of person. If anything, I go against the flow. I don't flow at all. If a waterfall symbolizes going with the flow, then I would be the rock that sits under this waterfall. Following anything can be dangerous. I need to stop and think, analyze the issue from every angle before committing.

I need to stay safe.

For thousands of years Jews have been persecuted. I want to stay alive, keep things afloat, make sure my son makes it in this world.

Journal Entry #52

Train from Prague to Berlin, May 2005:
Before Ben was born, Jeremy and I travel to Berlin. No one in my family is excited that we're travelling to Germany. Jeremy's grandfather, who survived the Holocaust, said, "Berlin? Ech! What's there? There's nothing to see."

I have mixed feelings. I'm excited to see this vibrant city, teeming with art and culture. But it feels weird. Like there's a heaviness to it. So why in the world do I go?

Because I don't want to forget, but I would like to forgive. I want to remember, but I also want to look at Germany in a new way. In a way my grandparents and parents were never able, and are still not capable of doing. I want to look at the new generation and let them know I'm not angry with them. And I want to look into the eyes of the older generation and ask them questions: "What were you doing during the Second World War when my family was being murdered?"

I want to try and understand.

It's not easy travelling to a city steeped in such a horrific past. But just like most countries filled with atrocities (do countries exist that are not built on violence and suppression of other?), one has to look to the present and the future in order to move on, while at the same time always remembering.

Journal Entry #53

Post-Berlin visit, May 2005:

I've seen Berlin, witnessed its grand architectural feats, sampled currywurst, visited the Checkpoint Charlie Museum, saw the zoo, toured the lonely Jewish quarter and braved the Memorial to the Murdered Jews in Europe.

The size of the buildings and the massive architecture in Berlin dwarfed the small, colourful buildings in the old town of Prague, where Jeremy and I spent our first week of holiday. In Berlin, I felt small and uncomfortable, as if I didn't belong there, as if the imposing buildings were coming alive, eyes watching my movements as I scurried along the streets like an animal running from danger.

Everything was large and loud in Berlin. But when we arrived in the Jewish quarter, it was so quiet and nondescript I didn't know we were standing in the middle of it until I looked at my guidebook. Everything Jewish was almost invisible. Even the synagogue we visited looked like every other concrete building on the block, with the exception of a small star on the outside. The large doors were locked tight and there was an intercom system with rows of buttons and I wondered how Jews could keep living here, among the ghosts.

By 1945, two out of every three Jews in Europe had been murdered. How did survivors go back? How did my own grandparents go back to a place that killed all of their family and so many of their people? How could these places still feel like home?

As we stood among the concrete slabs at the Memorial to the Murdered Jews in Europe, my body tightened with fear. How could these slabs of concrete make up for the six million?

I couldn't stay there. I didn't want to. Jeremy and I both wished we had made our trip shorter than the six days we stayed. We almost changed our tickets.

Sometimes when I travel to a place I get this feeling and I say to myself, yup, I don't ever have to come back here again.

I felt it.

In my gut.

I knew I wouldn't be back.

July 13, 2016

Dear Ben,

The wind whispers through trees and whistles past ears. The arbutus drop their flowers and leaves in the spring, their bark and fruit in the fall. One summer we stand on the deck and we paint, you, bare-chested boy belly on one side of canvas, me on the other. I pretend I'm a painter, an artist, and I stare at the Salish Sea, at the foamy whitecaps, until my eyes blur and it looks as though the water is moving in all directions. There is a surge of restlessness in my body, an unsettling. I don't finish the painting and the canvas remains incomplete and I don't touch it the next summer.

This house. Filled with the sound of children running barefoot and squealing to the sound of the trumpeting kingfishers, the echo of ravens calling in the tall cedar. This is your place, your freedom, the great outdoors.

And yet.

And yet you'd always rather be inside. Always at home. Safe and tucked away.

It's remarkable how the beauty of earth can feel so threatening.

When you hear a noise, your body holds still, seized like a deer in the woods. Your ears are like two giant sound-detecting saucers and you're able to hear things that others do not.

It's a skill. A gift.

But you don't sleep.

And your heart knows there are ghosts in the wind that shuffles between the trees. You hear the voices and watch them whip waves into whitecaps across ocean channel and into cove.

A click of a mousetrap followed by peals of squeaking, only heard by those with large saucer ears.

The walls in this house are alive.

In the morning you get up to check the trap and all you see is a severed paw.

Love always,
Mom

Journal Entry #59

On a website that lists ninety important facts about the Holocaust, number sixteen defines it as: *A sacrifice, in which a whole animal is burned.* It's derived from the Greek words *holos* or *whole* and *kaustos, to burn.*

Millions taken, gassed and burnt. Bodies incinerated. Ash falling from sky.

A sacrifice.

What god was Hitler trying to please?

July 25, 2016

Dear Ben,

How do I tell you about my heart? Do I let you know the fear that surrounds its muscles, causing the organ to seize periodically throughout the day? Or that sometimes just thinking about you brings this sadness so large I'm scared it will break me?

Do I let you know that as a girl I grew up with my heart wrapped in stone, layers and layers, each glued down with cement, my shoulders hunched over just to carry its weight?

How do I prevent any of these traumas from being imprinted on you when everything has already been stamped on egg and sperm at the moment of conception, memories of events passed down through generations?

I might just have to give up.

The thing is, your genes carry memories of where they come from. The body is wise in this way. It's the brain that is slow to catch up.

When I listen to your fears, they are mine. When I see your struggles, they are mine. When your hands make fists to punch me, they are mine. When your voice rages, it is mine. I am so scared I gave you everything. All of me. And the ghosts. So many of them. They're a part of you. And it all came in a package of transgenerational light switches. The clicking, on and off, of genes.

And we remember.

We carry this memory in our bodies.

And we will never forget.

Love always,
Mom

Journal Entry #64

I read Holocaust books and my spine twitches, like I'm getting ready to run. My senses are supersonic, triple in sensitivity. When I am alone and there is the slightest sound, I stop breathing so I can listen. I am alarmed. My heart is chronically clenched, thudding in my chest, and I gulp air to avoid tears. I feel like crying all the time. I've been having nightmares. In the morning, Jeremy tells me he heard my gasps of breath, flailing limbs, jumbles of words.

Holocaust scholar Terrence Des Pres quotes British novelist, A. Alvarez, saying that the immersion in Holocaust literature coincides with his personally knowing half a dozen suicides or near suicides.

My friends and family worry about me.

They tell me to balance the darkness with light. I listen. I stop reading books about the Holocaust at night and take up some lighter fiction instead, although I'm drawn to the dark. I make sure to get outside, to play with Ben, to see friends. But the stories of my family and other survivors are always there and I feel as if something is missing if I'm not writing or reading about their experiences. Sometimes it feels as though I'm inside something that no one else can see.

MY MOTHER, MY FATHER, MY SISTER AND I gather around my babi's hospital bed and watch her dying.

How the nurse comes in and wipes her mouth with a damp swab. How she says, "It won't be long now." How my family stands in a huddle at the foot of my babi's bed. How I sit beside her and hold her hand. How I rub my fingers over her wrinkled translucent skin. How her warm hand sits limp in mine. How puffs of air breathe in and out of her mouth, but the pauses between grow longer.

How helpless we feel as we watch her die. How restless the helplessness feels. When we can't stand it anymore, we go for a walk in a big, leafy neighbourhood. We file past mansions, castle-like fortresses of old Vancouver, and our hearts hang at the bottoms of our feet. Cellphones are on just in case.

We are waiting for my babi to die.

It feels strange walking in the beauty of this neighbourhood, hot summer sun and trees as wide as houses, when my babi's dying in a hospital bed a few blocks away.

My family does a loop and heads back down the hill. My body feels light, as if my feet aren't touching the ground. We take the elevator up and return to the foot of my babi's bed. Her breathing has changed. She's gasping, and we watch. There is such a long pause between the breaths we don't know which one will be her last. I go out to find the nurse and when I come back, my babi exhales her last breath. It sounds like a heavy sigh. And then it's over. Her chest does not rise again. The nurse checks her pulse and nods. I look at my mother, my father. My sister has a hand over her mouth, the other on her stomach. My father takes my mother's shoulders. My sister and I stand close to my parents. I open a window. I remember hearing about how the spirit needs a place to go.

My family and I emerge from the room as though we've been underground without food or water for a week. The halogen lights in the hallway are too bright. *Have they always been this bright?* We take the elevator down. I stand near the front desk.

"Someone must have just passed away," the receptionist says. "The door alarm went off and no one was there. It always happens when someone dies." I stare at the receptionist and tell him that my grandmother is dead.

"I'm so sorry," he says.

I walk outside to find my family. There is a dime on the ground and I pick it up and put it in my pocket. I see my sister sitting on a bench. We sit together in silence and watch the movement of the world outside. A butterfly sits on a rhododendron bush, orange and black wings open and close. My body is still numb when I notice a squirrel. The squirrel pauses and looks at me, whiskers aquiver. I smile and shake my head because I know. I know it's my grandmother. I know my grandmother is here with me.

August 4, 2016

Dear Ben,
Today I signed you up for summer day camp at the community centre and I thought about how the term *concentration camp* sounds more like a board game than hellish death prisons.

Love always,
Mom

THE WINTER OF 2015 I couldn't sleep for three months. Something was simmering inside me, moving just below my skin, keeping me awake. I was restless, irritable, a royal bitch, and I was making my family miserable. I switched around my vitamins, took more hormones, got a prescription for two types of sleeping pills. Nothing worked. I still woke up multiple times a night. I'd lie there next to Jeremy, listening to his gentle waves of breath, watching the shadows as they slowly crossed the ceiling above my bed. Early in the morning, just before dawn, I could see my panic. Thick and black like tar, my panic expanded and pinned me to my mattress. Pulse and mind racing, stomach lurched. It held me down until my alarm rang.

I bought one of those SAD lights, thinking the oppressiveness of Vancouver's wet winter was starting to get to me. After three weeks of diligent use and no change, I returned the light. I went to a natural health store and told an herbalist about my insomnia. She asked if anyone I was close to had died recently. "My grandmother," I said, "but it was six months ago—does that count?" and she said, "Of course, it counts." And so she gave me a remedy for grief in the form of tea.

I didn't know what to do or who to turn to. Sitting meditation wasn't doing anything. I needed to move.

A friend had told me about dynamic meditation and how amazing it is for shifting stuck energy. One night after Ben was asleep and Jeremy was out of town, I went downstairs in my pajamas, made some grief tea and decided to look it up. There were five steps so I rolled down the blinds, turned on some fast-paced drum music and started moving.

I began with my feet firmly planted on the floor, breathing in and out through my nose, knees bending up and down to the rhythm of the drums. This went on for ten minutes or so and then I stopped to read the next instructions.

I was supposed to dance around with my eyes closed and scream. Because Ben was sleeping upstairs, I decided to muffle my cries by screaming into a pillow. I only let out a few bellows, but I didn't feel any immediate release. Actually I felt a little silly. So I stuck to the hysterical dancing. I went crazy, my eyes squinting to make sure I didn't crash into the kitchen counter or the table. I spun, kicked, jumped and got down on all fours, thrashing. My tears found me.

The next part was jumping up and down, and letting out breath, and I did this until I felt I couldn't do it anymore. Then I turned the music off and sat on my meditation cushion. I brought my hands to my stomach and then moved them away from me, as though I was pushing something out of my body that I didn't want there anymore. I repeated this motion faster and faster, my tears streaming. I then saw my grandmother, bent and crooked, float above me. And she was dying. Even though it didn't look like her, I knew it was. She was emaciated and struggling.

"Babi," I said. "You're free now. You don't have to suffer anymore. You can go."

Then my hands pushed her out and she floated up and I let her go. And so I sat there, as this was the next stage in the meditation anyhow, and I caught my breath. The last part was dancing euphorically and although I wasn't feeling euphoric, I closed my eyes and swayed.

That night I slept the sleep of a dead woman.

August 16, 2016

Dear Ben,

We are lying in your bed snuggling and you let me put my cold hands on the soft oven of your nine-year-old belly.

"They're not too cold," you say. "You can warm them up on me."

Your skin is so smooth, I take my other hand and put it there too. Your body twitches in shivers and then you giggle. "Put your whole head under the tent, Mom," you say. "You'll warm up faster."

I do as I'm told and we talk softly together under the shadow of the blankets in your bedroom.

"I'm cold," you say, suddenly. I tell you I'm sorry for stealing your warmth and then I wrap my arms around you, and we spoon together until you shift in a way I know means you've had enough.

"I'm hotter than before," you say as we both lift our heads to let in the sweet cool air. I slowly remove myself from your blanket and tuck you in. And then I sit on the edge of your bed and rest a hand on your back.

And I think about the mothers and the children in the concentration camps. How they were torn apart and murdered separately. How one watched the other get shot or bludgeoned to death. How they were taken to the gas chambers, together, for their last breaths.

Love always,
Mom

ONE NIGHT BEN TELLS ME I look sad. Sometimes, even though he's only nine, he can feel my emotions before I can. I am restless as I put him to bed.

I notice the moon is full and round through the window in his room. There is a large bang that comes from the hallway and my adrenaline kicks in. Ben's ears send out their sonar.

"What was that?" he asks, ducking under the covers.

"I'm not sure," I say. "It's probably just the heat clicking on."

He stays under the covers and I join him there. I know he can hear the ghosts too. He squeezes his two lambies tight and brushes one of their ears against his nose, the way he used to when he was little.

Jeremy is out. I leave a light on upstairs so I'm not as frightened. My body leads. It knows what it wants and how it wants to move. I don't turn on any music. I freestyle.

I dance around in my living room, vigorously, trying to shake my body free from whatever it's holding onto. I collapse on the rug and stare at the ceiling, my breath heaving from exertion. The ceiling is white—flat, a canvas sky. I'm still trembling from all my whirling; even my eyes are shaking, and this makes the ceiling tremble too. Then I allow my body to calm down and my breath to slow and the ceiling stops moving. There is a shiny glow of warm light. Then I see *his* face. An image of my děda. He is wearing his houndstooth cap. He is smiling. I can see the sadness in his eyes.

Even though I'm scared, even though I want to, I don't push him away. I let him be there with me until his face becomes blurry. I feel the outer corners of my eyes grow wet.

When Jeremy comes home, I don't tell him about my děda. I don't tell him about the dancing or the breathing or the wet corners of eyes. We watch *Saturday Night Live* bloopers and we get ready for bed and we sleep. I don't tell him about the ghosts.

Journal Entry #67

I am lying face up under my white duvet with a warm heating pad filled with wheat berries pressed against my abdomen. I breathe in. The heating pad smells like lavender. I have just popped two more painkillers. I have also just finished a weekend filled with rage. This is typical with Premenstrual Dysphoric Disorder (PMDD), which I was diagnosed with a year after Ben's birth. I often describe it as a case of Dr. Jekyll and Mrs. Hyde. One moment I'm fine, the next I snap. Things that don't usually bug me will set me off. The loud drumming of Ben's foot against the kitchen counter. Jeremy playing guitar too early in the morning, singing the same song over and over again. Someone forgetting to change the toilet paper. A wet towel left on the floor. These tiny little things, which might get an audible sigh during the average week, with PMDD receive a thunderous explosion. These explosions are usually followed by feelings of remorse followed by apologies. When I get my period, Dr. Jekyll miraculously returns.

There is currently no cure for PMDD. One doctor describes PMDD, as PMS on steroids and another says it's often mistaken for bipolar disorder. Five percent of the population has PMDD, and new research revealed that PMDD might be genetic. Which means I've inherited an irregularity in the way my genes express. A part of me knows this disorder is connected with the trauma of Ben's birth, but also with the trauma of my family's history. The articles tell me my cells are more sensitive, that I respond atypically to changes in sex hormones, that I'm biologically different. Perhaps this new research will mean people will actually believe me when I tell them this isn't all in my head. That maybe people will finally be able to understand.

THE FACT MY SON HAD NO BREATH when he was born. I repeat this to myself, to other people, a story I tell—again and again because sometimes it's hard to believe, hard to digest. I repeat it as a way to grieve what happened. Yet the grief hasn't hit me until now. My body has slowly revealed this information to me over the last nine years of Ben's life. Adrenal fatigue. Hypothyroidism. Premenstrual Dysphoric Disorder. Insomnia. Clenching, body tight, protecting itself from further wounding, yet in this protection it has been unable to heal itself. Fortified by the birth trauma, these thick walls of defense have prevented my body from returning to a place of equilibrium.

Why am I only feeling the effects of this grief now? Was it because my son survived and so I didn't have to grieve? But I did. Oh, how I had to. How I wish I had made room for grief.

I had to grieve the loss of a beautiful home birth. The grief of a baby in distress. The grief of knowing I should have gone to the hospital even when the midwives said to wait. The grief of being strapped to a chair and hauled out my front door into bursts of sunshine by our neighourhood team of firefighters and first responders. The grief of sucking into an oxygen mask, unable to push because each time I did, my baby's heart rate decelerated. The grief of blinding lights, a nurse barking. The grief of an incision through my abdomen, and another through my uterus, a baby pulled out, limp, without breath. A husband not knowing who to be with and which way to go. A baby hooked up to machines. His kidneys shutting down. His other organs also failing. Grief of not holding him, not being there for the first moments of his life. Grief that he was alone, without his mother. Grief that the first thing that coursed through his body was the acrid taste of antibiotics rather than his mother's milk.

When I returned home from the hospital, I was alone with my baby. I nursed him, held him. Felt relief that he was okay. Felt gratitude to all those who had helped. Felt compassion for those who were still suffering. And I kept going. Like I was preparing for battle. Sleep, wake, feed, sleep, wake, feed. There was no time for feeling anything except the utter exhaustion of a new mother.

That I am now feeling the deep sadness and grief of Ben's birth nine years ago means that I am finally ready to heal. I know if I don't deal with the trauma now, I risk hurting myself further, my body and my spirit.

Journal Entry #72

I have spent most of the day indoors. When I reach my parents' house, the winter sun is still shining and I feel the pull to be outside. The door swings open and it's my father with a newspaper in his hands. I hear my mother in the kitchen, the faucet running.

"Hi," I say to my father. "Feel like going for a walk?"

My father shrugs and sits back down in his chair by the window. My mother comes out of the kitchen and wipes her wet hands on her pants. We kiss each other on the cheek.

"Where should we walk?" she asks.

"Somewhere in the sun," I reply.

Winters on the coast in the Pacific Northwest are soggy and oppressively grey. When the sun does make an appearance in Vancouver, the city suddenly bursts alive with people coming out of hibernation to enjoy the break from the rain. Sometimes it feels like I'm a vampire—when the sun appears after weeks of hiding, it's so bright I have to shield myself from exposure.

"The cemetery is always sunny," my mother says. "Dead people have the best real estate."

I don't like cemeteries. It's not that I fear the dead or think zombies will come crawling out of the ground, but I don't believe people stay where we bury them. And if people aren't actually there, then why can't we just visit them anywhere? On top of a mountain, on an ocean, in houses or cars.

My mother has a strong fascination with cemeteries but she doesn't think it has anything to do with the fact that she lost most of her family in the Holocaust. She says she likes cemeteries because they are so bright and most have great views. "Cemeteries are like huge, open, park-like spaces," she says. "They're quiet, peaceful and full of history."

In Prague my mother lived across from two cemeteries—one Jewish, the other Christian. They are the largest cemeteries in Prague. My babi's father, Vilém, who died of a brain tumour just before the war, is buried there. Author Franz Kafka is buried there too, and so is Jan Palach, a Czechoslovakian student who set himself on fire to protest the Soviet invasion of 1968.

It was my mother's idea to apply for her first summer job as a teenager at the Christian cemetery with her friend Lida. The Christian cemetery was much larger, so my mother thought they'd have a better chance of getting jobs. Together they cleaned the graves and paths. They dragged bulky hoses around to water the plants on the graves. They cut the overgrown ivy off the headstones and swept the leaves and branches. Sometimes elderly women would give them a few Czech crowns for taking care of their relatives' graves. They worked at the cemetery together for two summers. During their lunch breaks, they'd sit on the framed edges of gravestones so they wouldn't desecrate them. My mother would have dry old bread with Hungarian salami, while Lida ate fried-egg sandwiches.

Later my parents would move into their house, one block away from a cemetery. This is where my grandparents would be buried.

It would be another forty years until Jeremy, Ben and I moved into a house with a cemetery at the end of the road.

MOURNING THE DEAD gets complicated when there is little or no information on when or where people died. Family members were taken and disappeared. Although the Nazis kept impeccable records, they destroyed so many of them toward the end of the war in order to hide evidence of genocide. There were no bodies to mourn, no graves to attend to, no death certificates issued. There was no closure. In many cases, as was with my grandparents, survivors didn't find out about what happened to other members of their families until months after liberation. To survive the horrors of the death camps, and then to be told that they were the sole surviving members of their families, as was the case with both my babi and děda, to mourn adequately would have been too overwhelming.

After the war, many survivors wanted to move forward with their lives, find a new home, create families. My grandparents didn't want to stay stuck in the past; they didn't want to relive the horrors. They might have been afraid that their sadness would engulf them. There was no one to talk to. They had only each other. So they delayed their grief. They delayed it, but it kept finding them again and again until my děda couldn't cope. His grief was like a tsunami, and it knocked him over and cut him down. I think about my grandparents' apartment. I imagine myself looking out their living room window as I so often have in the past, and I can see the Salish Sea, wedged between buildings. When he jumped, it's as if he was looking for this body of water, so it could catch him, and break his fall.

Journal Entry #75

My therapist friend once described my personality as melancholic. I immediately pictured Eeyore from Winnie the Pooh. The head bent, staring at the floor, down in the dumps donkey.

Although I don't consider myself melancholic, I am attracted to melancholy. I seem to gather friends who have experienced a wide assortment of grief. A parent who died young, a sibling's suicide, a family fleeing from war. This grief is often not discussed but rather felt, as if these relationships were formed at a subconscious level. As if we're connected via our collective grief. Together we have discussions, many which focus on death and dying. It is comforting to be able to speak openly about death, especially in a society that shuns such conversations.

ON DECEMBER 17, the day before my babi would have turned 104, we go out for Chinese food with my parents. The street is slick like ink and the rain beats down in large drops, and Ben asks me to turn the wipers on high. Jeremy and I have just had an argument but I can't remember what it was about. I woke up feeling angry. In December, I often do. There is one parking spot left at the back of the restaurant and I drive by it so my parents can park there—they live twenty minutes away and might be stuck in traffic. I turn right out of the alley and find a spot on the side of the road.

We jump out of the car and run half a block to the restaurant. The door opens with a tinkle of bells. A man and woman behind the bar greet us and the woman walks toward us with menus. I scan the restaurant. My parents have not yet arrived.

We grab a table and Ben keeps his hood on. He gazes at the TV at the other end of the restaurant. There's a curling match on. The TV is like a magnet and he is gone. I order some herbal tea and it comes in a bud. I pour hot water on it and watch the flower unfold, its petals dancing, alive.

My parents walk in a few minutes later. My mother is at the door, shaking off her umbrella. My father takes off his hood and then unzips his green jacket. They are smiling when they come to the table. They order tea and we pick up the menu and discuss what to order. I'm not sure why we do this, because we usually order the same dishes no matter what Chinese restaurant we go to: ginger beef, chicken chow mein, orange peel chicken, Buddha's feast. Tonight, just to be different, we order the hot and sour soup because we are cold. Because my insides refuse to warm up.

We chat about wild weather and climate change around the world, a favourite topic of Ben's. Hurricane Patricia with winds gusting up to 345 kilometres an hour. Record-breaking heat waves across continents. Warming oceans.

Then my parents turn to politics. The discussion stays neutral, steers away from the personal. Terrorism in Europe, the Syrian refugee crisis. Toward the end of dinner, no one has mentioned my grandmother, the reason we are gathered on this dreary winter night.

I clear my throat. "I think we should talk about Babi," I say. My parents and my husband look at me.

"What about her?" my mother asks.

"Well, I kind of pictured us going around the table and telling stories about her," I say. "Like how she loved Chinese food. Remember when we used to go to Cleveland Dam to the restaurant near the mountain and she would order the sweet-and-sour deep-fried prawns. How the yellow breading was so thick and the cherry red sauce so bright, and the prawn seemed so tiny when we'd finally found it, it was as if we'd won a prize."

"I don't remember that," says my mother.

"All these questions, all this remembering has been so hard on your mother," my father says.

The conversation steers back to politics. I pick up my tea. It is cold.

After dinner, safe back home, my anger melts into sadness. There's a well of tears pooled in the pit of my stomach. But they never make it up to my face and out of my body. Later, I check my email and there's a message from my mother. She tells me she's sorry the dinner didn't turn out the way I had intended. That she wasn't in the mood to remember. That grief hits everyone at different times. That it can't be forced or planned. That her grief still comes and goes.

That I am not alone in mine.

Journal Entry #82

I'm travelling to a writing conference in Los Angeles with a good friend in a couple of weeks and I'm already dreading the departure. It's not the fear of flying but the actual physical separation part that terrifies me. What if something happens to Ben? To Jeremy? What if they die? If I don't leave, I believe there's a better chance they will survive. Yet I know it's important to have space. So I panic. I make lists for Jeremy.

Friday: Feed fish. Pack lunch (pizza, veggie, fruit, snack), water bottle, winter jacket, snow boots (if needed). Bring PE strip in backpack. Take vitamins (in fridge and cupboard). Practise drums. Do homework. Check mail. There is chili in fridge for dinner.

Saturday: Feed fish. Vitamins. Soccer game at 9 a.m. Bring cleats, shin guards, uniform, water bottle. Put cold gear on underneath if needed. Bring hat and gloves. Location: Thunderbird Stadium. Practise drums. Take shower. Lentil soup in fridge.

Sunday: Feed fish. Vitamins. Practise drums. Water plants. Grandma is coming over to visit at 10 a.m. Please make her a coffee. Please put all dirty laundry in hamper. I will be landing at 3:47 p.m. Should be home by 5 p.m.-ish.

Then I list emergency numbers: my parents, Ben's doctor and his school.

Once the lists are finished, I print them out and put them on the counter. Then I leave. But I never really want to go.

IT IS THE DEAD BLACK of winter. I am driving and the car is full with Jeremy, Leah and Ben. Our collective breathing fogs up the windshield and I blast the fan. We are driving to visit our family friends, and my parents are coming too. Leah is talking about registering for a kickboxing class and tells me I should sign up. I picture the two of us in boxing gloves, releasing whatever pent-up anger we have stored, and decide it's a good idea. When we get to Ted and Shirley's house, another car pulls up and a big bush of curly hair pops out of the driver side. When he sees us, Frank's face breaks into a smile. Frank is Ted and Shirley's son; he has just moved back home after being away for ten years, and we are celebrating his return. We take turns hugging him in big fleecy bear hugs. Ben watches his own breath blow warm into the frost-covered night.

Inside, Ted and Shirley ask me about the book I'm working on. I fill them in and tell them about my depression. That the last couple of months have been difficult, full of fear. But I don't tell them about how my eyes pop open well before my six o'clock alarm and how a surge of cold panic sweeps through me. I don't know what to do with this rush of feelings so I just lie there, helpless. It feels like a wave that could swallow me whole. Sometimes I make myself feel it, and sometimes when I do, I am able to disperse it a little. Sometimes it's so intense I need to get up and brush my teeth, take a shower, get dressed, make coffee and put the dishes away.

I do tell them about my grandmother's birthday on December 18, about how she hated celebrating it because it reminded her of the deportations to the death camps. I don't tell them about how in November my body begins to shiver and that by December my insides are frozen, how darkness reaches out to me with a long, crooked finger, urging me to follow.

When we finish dessert and it's time to leave, I go into the kitchen to thank the hosts. They are cleaning up. Ted is wearing a red apron and has a yellow tea towel draped over one shoulder. When they see me, their eyes show concern.

"Isn't there a way to turn it around and not feel victimized?" Ted asks. "What about the fact they survived? That they built this life, here, a beautiful life for their daughter and family?"

I appreciate their concern. I don't tell them about my grandfather's suicide. They don't know about some of the dark. It's not the place to share this information.

"I agree about feeling victimized. I desperately want not to feel this way. But I think I have to go through it. Walk through this fire before I can come out the other side. I need to feel like a victim before I can let it go."

They nod and we exchange hugs.

"Thanks for dinner," I say. "And for the kindness and concern."

I gather my family and we walk out into the frosty night.

"There's Venus," Ben says, pointing to the sky.

I smile and nod, and as my arms wrap around him, I burrow my face in his neck and breathe him in.

BOOK FOUR

"What do you do with what happened to you? Do you just carry that trauma and pain around with you your whole life or is there a way, this is my eternal question, is there a way to compost it and turn it into something useful?"

—Lidia Yuknavitch
"The Way Forward with Lidia Yuknavitch"
Lit up (podcast) Chapter 15: July 21, 2015

"Every trauma provides an opportunity for authentic transformation."

—Peter A. Levine
Waking The Tiger: Healing Trauma
North Atlantic Books, 1997

THE WAITING ROOM is white. Bright walls and clean lines. Two women sit behind the reception counter and one of them greets me by name. I read the labels of the organic products on display and examine the assortment of raw and vegan books on the shelf beside them. I sit down on the green chairs and flip through my phone. My friend has added a new video of her kid on Facebook and I watch him walk for the first time, his movements stiff like Frankenstein. My face breaks into a smile.

The doctor comes out. She is dressed in a fancy suit and looks impeccable, as usual. Her hair is cut into a short bob and she has glasses that make her eyes look big, like an owl. She pushes them up the bridge of her nose and smiles.

"Hello," I say.

She nods and watches me stand up and walk toward her. She is giving me the once over, making sure I haven't lost any hair or my body hasn't changed since she saw me last.

The first time she checked me out she asked me if I was balding, as if I knew I was losing my hair. I have a ton of it, big bushes of dark brown curl, and it's always falling out. I had no idea I could be losing it. "What?" I said, as if I hadn't heard her. But inside, my mind was racing, my body going into its habitual numbed state, the way it does when anything shocks me. Going bald would be one of those things. I kept quiet while she touched my scalp, and then sat down.

That was three years ago. In her office I heard these words for the first time: hypothyroid, adrenal fatigue, low progesterone and cortisol irregularity.

Three years later we are still trying to figure my body out.

"I think we're doing all that we can," she says, after I tell her about my latest bad menstrual cycle.

"There must be something else," I say.

I am desperate. I tried antidepressants once for a few months when I was first diagnosed with PMDD. Instead of helping, they messed up my insides. My moods stayed the same.

"We've got your thyroid covered and you're taking vitamins for your adrenals. No," she says. "I think that's it."

She watches me with her large owl eyes and my heart grows heavy, begins to sink.

"I think it's time you investigated your head," the doctor says.

I turn away and scratch the top of my skull. I look at her bookshelf and read the spines of the thick medical textbooks. Words like balance and hormone and gut, holistic, integrative and nutrition.

"We've talked about the mind/body connection before," she says. "You could be taking all the pills in the world and nothing would change if your mind doesn't want it to."

"Are you saying I'm doing this to myself?" I ask.

She raises both eyebrows and her forehead wrinkles. She adjusts her glasses and smiles. "Don't think of it like that," she says. "Everything works on an energetic level. There are things we can't begin to understand. We're talking quantum physics. Ever hear the expression, 'Some things can't be explained'? This is one of them."

I fiddle with a hangnail.

"I'll give you this woman's website. She's an energy healer of sorts. I called her up and we had a Skype session. I have to say I felt better afterward and so I feel okay recommending her," she says.

"You Skyped? Don't you need to see her in person?" I ask.

The doctor stares at me and it feels likes her retinas are trying to drill holes into my corneas. "Energy knows no bounds," she replies.

The doctor types the healer's name and website on her laptop and presses print.

"Don't come back until you've tried it," she says.

This feels as though I'm being kicked in the ass. I am shocked and I don't react. Instead she hands me the paper and I thank her. She turns back to her computer and starts typing again. On the wall above her computer, there's a landscape painting—a mountain range drawn in black ink. It is stark, and against the white wall, it looks empty, like it has been waiting a long time for the colours to come.

I put my jacket on and say goodbye and then close the door behind me. I fold the paper in half and wait a month before I email the healer.

Healer #1

It's a hot day in July and Ben is at soccer day camp with his best friend. I make the appointment for ten in the morning so I don't get stuck in traffic on the highway. I drive forty-five minutes to get to the healer's townhouse without a GPS and am relieved to arrive with only mild anxiety. She opens the door and she pulls me in with her brown eyes, like two magnetic orbs. The house smells like lavender. As we enter her kitchen, I notice the diffuser steaming on the counter. The healer's long, straight hair hangs like two brown curtains framing her oval face, and with her chiselled features she looks like a sculpture.

"Is that lavender?" I ask.

"Yes," she says, pointing to the diffuser.

"I love that smell," I say. "I find it so calming. I have a diffuser too but I never use it. I mean I used to but then I forgot about it and now it's sitting in a drawer somewhere and I'd have to search for it and clean it out with rubbing alcohol. Too much maintenance. Especially when it's supposed to stress you out less and not more."

I babble the way I normally do when I meet someone for the first time. Instead of remembering a name or asking questions, I'll talk about the weather and how punctual I always am, but what I'm really doing is focussing on making sure I'm not drooling or that the dress I'm wearing isn't tucked into my underwear.

We go downstairs to a library with a massage table set up by the window. There is new-agey music playing that reminds me of the music many practitioners of alternative medicine play, trying to be calming, but mostly working to irritate me instead. I sign a waiver, which I skim because she's talking, and I'm nervous so I have no idea what I've just committed to.

"Sorry, I know this is going fast," she says. "It's the way I operate. Things come rushing at me and I either go with them or decide not to in that moment. Please feel free to ask questions and stop me at any time."

I look at her pupils, which are now even bigger; two large mud puddles, they appear to spin to hypnotize me.

She talks of energetic clearing on a quantum level, that we are used to vibrating in a certain place, and that it takes a lot of work for us to shift because we want to hold on to the old stuff—we don't want to let go.

She gestures a lot with her long arms and talks about angels and breathing and anger that is ancient, older than me.

"This is trapped anger," she says. "It's really old cellular anger that got stuck."

"Stand up and come over here," she says, directing me to the middle of the room.

She places her hands on my diaphragm. "Now breathe in and out," she says.

I freeze a little as she touches me and I can feel her cold hands through my shirt. I breathe in.

"See how little your diaphragm actually expands? You're not getting enough oxygen. Things are being compressed," she says, as I exhale slowly.

"Now put your hands on my ribs," she says.

"Is this going to be homework?" I ask.

I feel her ribs protrude through her skinny frame.

"Yes," she says. "This is a way of working on connecting with the body from the inside. Watch as I begin by pulling my breath up through my vagina to my heart centre."

She breathes and the whole centre of her body expands, as if she were getting ready to fill a huge balloon.

When she is done I sit back down on the couch and she talks about my healing, and how my son and husband will also be supported on my journey, how she's looking out for all of us. She says I should be asking archangels Michael and Raphael for guidance and that she's clearing energy by working directly with my spine, running along each vertebra. I begin to understand the spine to be something that reaches through the ground and up through the heavens, with no beginning and no end, kind of like a tree.

Mostly when she talks, I'm overwhelmed and sit in the fog of my silence. Occasionally, my foot will tap or I'll pinch the skin of my hand. I don't know if she notices. While she speaks, I look between my feet and see a dime and reach down to pick it up. I put it on the table in front of her.

She stops talking and stares at the dime before she looks up at me with her eyes wide, and asks, "Did your grandmother die?"

I never told her about my babi's death, so I'm not sure how she knows this. Maybe she asks all her clients if their grandmothers have died and maybe she is only right half the time.

"She died almost a year ago," I say.

"She's with you," she says. "She wants you to know that it's okay to let go. That she's fine with all this, your desire to stop holding on to these rigid ways of being, the old familial pattern of control."

I have tears in my eyes and I nod because I can feel my grandmother.

I am amazed with how much this healer knows about me. She knows both my son and I don't like loud noises, that I get overwhelmed by people, even those I love. She understands my rage, how it courses through me, hot lava bursting through my skin. And she knows about how much burden I feel, how serious and heavy my life is.

I look at her long, toned arms as they jolt around erratically, slicing the air up and down, and I notice a couple of yoga mats rolled up in the corner of the room.

"I'm giving you joy and humour because somehow you've lost these," she says.

I think about this and I know she's right. I do still have moments of joy. But I remember as a kid I used to laugh so hard my insides hurt—the kind of deep belly laugh that would last so long I'd have to pause to come up for air so I wouldn't pass out.

Then our time is up.

"You might feel some of the old anger. Remember your breath. There could be some sadness as well."

"But what if I don't feel anything?"

"I'm good at what I do," she says. "Oh, and your son should feel settled today."

"Great," I say.

When I get home I Google about finding dimes and I learn that the appearance of dimes and pennies is associated with a loved one who has recently passed away. I want to go back and tell the healer that I often find dimes. That I wish I could remember the last time I found one because it could have led me to my grandmother.

When I pick Ben and his friend up from day camp, they are both bouncing in the back seat of my car. Ben keeps pushing the button on the door that controls the window. Up, down. Up, down. His friend giggles then sneezes, and Ben laughs so hard he gets the hiccups. Before bed, Ben is spooked but he doesn't know why. He asks me to stay with him until he falls asleep.

"Of course," I say. "I love you so much."

"Mom, I didn't know this was possible, but I love you more every day."

He lies down and we spoon together and I whisper I love yous into his ear. He makes little-kid squeaks and snuggles with his lambies. I touch his matted brown curls as he drifts off to sleep.

Journal Entry #86

When I walk into Ben's room as I do every night before I go to sleep, I close the window a bit and tuck in his covers. The light from the hallway illuminates his sweet, rosy kid face, and even though he's nine years old, I lean down to make sure he's still breathing like I did habitually when he was a baby. When I see the rise and fall of his body and listen to his little sleep noises, I sit quietly beside him in the rocking chair and check in with my own body, with my own breath. And for a moment we stay like this, breathing together.

Healer #2

My sister tells me about EMDR, eye movement desensitization and reprocessing, a psychotherapy used for post-traumatic stress disorder. It's supposed to help people process traumatic memories by changing how they react to them. It is a therapy often used for soldiers with PTSD to help decrease the severity of traumatic memories and the negative emotions connected to them. I decide to see a healer who specializes in EMDR.

It's late summer when I walk into the healer's office. As I swing the door open, I discover mail scattered on the floor along with a rolled-up newspaper. I pick it up and call out for the healer, as I'm not positive I'm in the right place. She walks out of her office, into the hallway, and greets me with a warm smile. She has short white hair and her eyes are filled with understanding. I immediately feel comfortable with her. She's the kind of person I'd want to have tea with.

She invites me into her office, which is bright even with the blinds partially closed. There is a comfortable couch against the wall and I bring in my thermos filled with coffee. She sits opposite me in a big chair, with her foot up on a stool, a mug of hot water beside her. She tells me her leg has been bothering her and asks me if it's okay that she rests in this position for our session. "Of course," I say.

I want to dive right in but instead we tread lightly, get to know each other, a sort of dance. I tell her how I often feel guilty about my easy, soft life. How my struggles are small and meaningless in comparison to the generations preceding me.

"Wouldn't your grandmother have wanted you to have an easy life?" she asks.

"Yes," I say, remembering. "She often said she was glad things were so good for me. I'm not sure I ever thanked her for this life that I have. I should have."

"She's with you," the healer says. "And you're right. She would have wanted you to enjoy yourself."

"I can't stop feeling guilty though," I say. "I feel as though I need to suffer. I feel bad that my family had it so hard and I get off so easy. It's not fair. I think I'm making myself suffer. In my body—and my head."

After several sessions together over the course of a month, we finally broach the subject of Ben's birth, the trauma I've been wanting to work on and heal from. The healer takes what she calls a tapper, which looks like a small electronic box with wires coming out of it. I attach the ends to my legs with the Velcro straps. She starts the tapper and I feel a vibration pulsing repeatedly from one leg to the other. The vibrations are gentle and strangely calming. As she guides me, I follow my mind in quick flashes of memory. The bedroom. The doula. My midwives. Jeremy. Me crunching on an ice cube.

Me on all fours deep into labour. I am stuck on the part where I'm not listening to myself, my intuition, telling me to go to the hospital. Those bright flooding lights of the hospital room, the noise, the panic, the chaos. She stops the tapper and asks me to tell her what I'm seeing and feeling and then we continue.

Along with these painful images, I have other, more positive memories. Seeing Ben for the first time. Ben gripping my finger. Holding Ben. Feeding him. The warm smiles of the nurses in the NICU. The healer asks me to think of Ben and, when I do, I feel a fierce love that fills me to bursting.

When we finish our session, I walk back to my car. A seagull flies over my head and I watch it disappear over an apartment building. As I cross the street, a mother and her son head across toward me. He looks about three years old and is on his push bicycle and I watch his little legs run. He looks behind him and shrieks with delight when he sees his mother rushing to catch him.

Journal Entry #88

I listen to a podcast in which neuroscientist Rachel Yehuda tells me that just because we're each born with a certain set of genes, we are not necessarily in biological prisons. We have the capacity to change how these genes function. She says we have the ability to carry our trauma with us in a way that honours our past, in a way that doesn't have to overtake us. She says we can learn to carry our trauma forward and not be tormented by it, but turn it into something positive instead. I take a workshop led by the brilliant author and cheerleader of misfits, Lidia Yuknavitch, and I'm already in tears when she tells me, "Your wound is your superpower."

Healer #3

I know that sometimes talking isn't enough. Just like sometimes sitting still doesn't help. I know I need to start paying attention to my body and the sensations produced within. I think of it as a portal into getting to know myself better, from the inside out, a way of connecting my mind to what I'm sensing. After the powerful experiences I had dancing and breathing and doing dynamic meditation in my living room, I figured any type of movement would generate some kind of internal response. Because my physical symptoms are still manifesting, my intuition is telling me to keep seeking, to keep trying healers to find the release my body needs.

My sister sends me an email for a healing group. It has to do with resetting the nervous system using TRE: Tension Releasing Exercises, a program designed by Dr. David Berceli, to release tension and encourage connection with the body. I email the healer and book a private session.

I show up wearing stiff jeans and when I see the healer wearing stretchy clothing, the kind that many healers wear, bright green organic hemp or bamboo with a turquoise scarf, I wish I had my exercise pants. She speaks in a gentle voice that sounds patronizing but I can see the kindness in her eyes. They are soft and sad, filled with her struggle and her compassion.

The room is bright and there is a yoga mat on the floor. I am nervous, the kind of feeling I get when I'm about to be observed. As she introduces herself, I look outside to the street below: I see the tall cedar nestled between houses, the crows meeting on the power line, the afternoon sun making moon-shaped slivers against the wall. The healer runs me through a series of exercises and then watches as I do them. She makes sure I am still breathing. When I hold a squat against a wall, my cheeks heat up.

"Just notice that," she says. "Pay attention to what's going on. This is your body beginning to release things."

When I do the last exercise, my body shakes from my torso all the way through to my feet. It's a strange sensation to feel my body convulse so involuntarily.

"The shaking comes from within," she says. "You're letting go of energy that needs to come out."

The healer says when she practises TRE, sometimes for an hour a day, her whole body shakes from head to toe. She says things will shift for me if I practise TRE a few times a week. That I'll notice a difference physically. That my cycles won't be so painful. I look at her and smile. I've heard so many healers say this to me over the last nine years. I don't believe her, but I know now that the answer lies within my body.

I pay twenty dollars for the pamphlet and learn that by nature our bodies are designed to let go of tension but, instead of shaking it off, we hold on to it and dissociate through freezing or numbing. This dissociation may help us get through the trauma short term but it means that tension remains in our bodies, even after the stressful event is over. This tension, unable to discharge fully, can lead to PTSD, intense emotions like rage and other illness.

This reminds me of the research done on behaviour in wild animals. Psychologist Peter Levine says wild animals enter an altered state in which they freeze when they sense a predator may be about to kill them. It's an involuntary survival strategy, and should a wild animal survive the danger, it will shake, and in this process, its body recovers and returns to its natural state of balance. This means the trauma of that moment has been released. The same applies to humans. However, because our modern culture sees this shaking or surrendering to tension as a sign of weakness, we tend to hold things in, freezing in fear but not releasing anything. It is through our freezing and lack of releasing that we create our traumatic symptoms.

I understand this to mean that it's essential for me to find my way back into my body. Energy has to move through me.

Holding on to it is making me sick. Trauma stays in the body and manifests as anxiety, depression and psychological and behavioural problems. We hold on to it because to let it out would make us look weak, uncivilized, messy. "We become victims of trauma," Levine says.

I practise TRE one evening a few days later. I've got two hours to myself, a rare occurrence. I walk myself through the series of exercises and at the end I shake. As I lie there, letting my body rattle away, I smile. It feels funny to watch my body shake. I play around with it, trying to stop the shaking with my brain, and I can't. The only way it will stop is if I physically change positions. It's wacky and kind of fun to watch my brain look at my body, and I see it as a greeting of sorts, a getting to know my physical self.

I think it's the first time I've ever slowed down enough to say hello.

August 19, 2016

Dear Ben,

I learn that I can teach you how to cope with your genetic imprinting. I can teach you how to feel things in your body. I can teach you that it's okay to feel sadness. To be in your body and feel pain. I can teach you to slow down, to listen to what your body is telling you, to listen to its wisdom. To sit with your panic, your anxiety. What does it feel like, Ben? What does it feel like to be in your body and where do you feel it most?

I can teach you that you can't change what happened to our family, or to you, but that you've got the present and the future. I can tell you that you're an empath and your sensitivities are a gift you can use to help others. That you need to take your wounds and use them to create beauty.

Love always,
Mom

Healer #4

She is German. I read the healer's biography online before I book. Her hair is light brown and cut to her shoulders. She is wearing a navy blue sweater with horizontal ribbing. She hasn't even sat down and I'm already telling her why I'm here. I tell her about how I'm holding things in my body. About the genocide. I don't name the Holocaust. Not right away. Because she's German and I don't want her to feel bad. So I tell her about my ancestors, that I was named after someone who was murdered, that my body is a tightly wound-up ball, about my periods and my thyroid, my fight-or-flight response, that I've been working to heal for a long time. When she speaks, her accent is thick. She doesn't tell me she is German. We both know what genocide I am talking about.

The healer begins with my feet. I'm lying face up under a sheet with an electric heating pad under my knees. Through two large windows, I have the most magnificent view of the forest. I watch the sunlight stream through the trees.

The healer touches my feet. "I can feel you're not in your body," she says. "But I can sense you're still here. That you're present."

I nod. "It feels like I'm buzzing about inside not totally connected to what's going on," I say.

I imagine my insides are kind of like a pinball. Where the ball pings around and my mind is trying to get a handle on it, make it do certain things, but the ball keeps zipping doing its own thing and my mind and body are just so far apart.

"What are your dreams like?" she asks.

"I don't remember most of them," I say. "Which is good because when I do, they're mostly nightmares."

"What are they about?" she asks.

"Last night I dreamt I was in a concentration camp," I say.

"You dreamt you were in a concentration camp?" she repeats.

"Yes. I was there. My grandmother was there too. But for some reason no one could see me, not even my babi. We were in the barracks. I was lying on the bottom bunk, with five others squished beside me. I could feel their shivering, their skeletal bodies pressing against me for warmth. My babi was by the window. Her head was shaved and the striped prison uniform hung from her starving body like a filthy rag. Suddenly there were German voices arguing. I ran to where my babi was standing and recognized the Nazi leaders, Himmler and Heydrich. They had just received orders to ramp up their killing efforts so that Jews could be murdered faster. Hitler didn't want one single Jew left alive and they weren't working fast enough. They were arguing about how to murder more people. I tried to grab my babi's arm to pull her away from the window. But my hands went right through her. Then an alarm went off."

"What happened?" the healer asks.

"It was my husband's cellphone ringing. His work was calling," I said. "The sweat was pouring from my body. I was relieved to be woken up."

On the table I am rigid. She pokes and kneads various body parts and sighs. "Your body feels like it's gone through major trauma," she says. "It feels as though you're holding back. That the answers are all there within you but for some reason you're not letting them out. It feels like this energy is stuck."

I listen with tears in my eyes. Because I know all this. She is not telling me anything new.

"I met this First Nations woman," she continues. "She travels around the world. She's a healer. She taught me about forgiveness. She said without forgiveness, we can't move forward. Instead we continue to carry the anger and grief in our bodies. She said without forgiveness, there is no way of letting go."

I look at her and know she is right.

It's August 2016, two years since my babi passed away. I haven't visited the cemetery, where they keep my děda's ashes, since I was little. My babi's ashes are there now too. It's off a main road, two blocks from where my parents live near Vancouver. I turn right and drive in through two iron gates. There are speed bumps to make sure I don't drive too fast. I park next to a black convertible that has a dream catcher hanging from the rear-view mirror. Two Remembrance Day poppies are attached to the visor.

The hedges are clipped neatly and the trees are pruned in a way that makes them look fake, too perfect. The main building is beige with green trim. There are flower baskets hanging in full bloom. The grass is green despite the summer lawn-watering restrictions.

The cemetery is called Cedar Lake even though there's no cedar and no lake. There is a small lily-filled pond though. There are pathways to the chapel, which are lined with trees. A small garden surrounds the pond, with benches and garbage cans. An airplane motors overhead, south, toward the airport. Across the street is a park where my sister and I used to run barefoot, chasing deer back into the forest.

I head toward the cemetery's main building. The blinds are white and drawn. The gravestones lie flat on the ground, interspersed with trees. The grass has been freshly cut. I open the door. There are two suit-wearing people sitting behind a counter; each one has a computer. It feels a bit like being in a principal's office.

"My grandparents are here," I say.

The woman stares at me while the man picks up a walkie talkie.

"Family services, location required please," he says into it.

"What are their names? How long ago did they pass away?" he asks.

I give him the information and he tells me to have a seat. There is a black leather couch facing the counter. I sit in the chair across from the door. I notice the bottom of the couch is worn. There is a box of Kleenex sitting on a glass coffee table. There are fake flowers and piles of newspapers. I try and look outside but the door's glass is frosted. There is an umbrella stand by the front door and tiles that lead to a green pastel carpet, worn like the couches. On a side table sits a colourful glass lamp that looks antique. On the counter there's an orchid and more Kleenex. I lock eyes with the woman and she doesn't smile. The air conditioning is blasting. I'm in shorts and a tank top but suddenly feel naked. Should I have dressed up?

A woman with a walkie talkie enters from down the hall. She is wearing a skirt suit, heels and heavy mascara.

"I was able to locate your grandparents," she says, smiling now. She hands me a map of the building and two other maps. One area of the map is circled in red. They are in section nine, inside the large building. I thank her and ask for directions since I can't read maps, and then she offers to take me there. I immediately accept since the last thing I want to do is get lost, wandering the hallways, surrounded by the ashes of dead people.

I tell her how I used to visit frequently as a child. That the marble sculpture of Moses with horns, a replica of Michelangelo's, used to freak me out. I didn't know at the time the horns were a result of a mistranslation of biblical Hebrew and were really meant to be rays of light. To the eight-year-old me, Moses looked like the devil.

"I never noticed the horns on Moses," she says. "I couldn't get past his arms."

I laugh at the thought of her staring at Moses' bulging biceps.

"My grandparents are here too," she says. "I used to come here all the time when I was young. Now I'm here even more."

We enter the large building. Then she leaves me, gives me the maps, and tells me to be well. There is a lump in my throat the size of a bullfrog and an ache in my jaw. My heart seizes and I try to catch my breath. My eyes tear for a second but I swallow hard and press them away.

It's too quiet to cry here.

I am standing in front of their rectangular copper nameplate. It says *LIPA*. Under *LIPA* are the first names of my grandparents along with their birthdates and the years they died. I do the math, for the first time realizing my děda was seven years older than my babi. The plaque sits on a red pedestal, protected by glass. Attached to the wall is a vase with flowers. The orchids are fake but the lavender is real, and I'm sure it comes from my mother's garden. She grows figs, blueberries and currants, peonies, tulips, daffodils, lilacs and so much more. In the warmer months her front yard looks like a magical kingdom.

I sit down by my grandparents' nameplate. A fruit fly circles my head. There is a large cross on the window. The tiles on the floor are beige. The white cushioned bench I sit on is frilly, with flowers on the pillows. It looks like it belongs outside on the deck of an old character home. A vacuum cleaner is tucked in a corner next to a folded mat. There are six rows of plaques and vases going up the wall, some with real flowers, some with fake ones, and some sit empty. There is a slight floral fragrance and when I glance up I notice there is an upstairs with more plaques and flowers.

Outside the window, an elderly man parks his pickup truck and walks on the grass between the rows of graves. He is wearing jeans and a button-up shirt and has pink roses and a bucket. A maintenance cart drives toward another building that looks like a small grey cathedral. There are rows of plum trees, and I wonder if they'd produce any fruit, and whether I'd ever eat plums from a cemetery. I think of Adam and Eve. I realize I have to pee. I notice that Moses sits in my grandparents' row. Jesus on the cross is in the row behind him. I walk out of the building and into the sun. A man weed whacks by the pond. He wears safety glasses and ear protection. I notice there are water striders gliding over the surface. I get into the car. I hold my pee.

I wait until I drive out of the cemetery before I cry.

Healer #5

I make an appointment with a shaman. I want to stop the ghosts of my ancestors from creating chaos inside me. They are with me all the time, wreaking havoc on my internal system. My Klára's face, pale and haunted. My babi's brother, Richard, his round glasses, his serious expression. My děda, his sad eyes, his houndstooth cap. My babi, waiting to die. I don't need them to go away, don't even know if that's possible, but I'd like stop carrying their weight, to stop my nervous system from going on overdrive, to allow my body and mind some peace. I don't know if I trust in all this energy work, but I think it's more that my brain doesn't like the things that it can't explain through science or fact. I know when I do go into these sessions, it's with an open heart, and practitioners have told me my body soaks everything up like a sponge. So screw my brain. I've been paying attention to the wrong body part for far too long.

I am nervous when I meet this shaman, just as my anxiety skyrockets when I meet anyone for the first time, and I sit beside her and fill out some forms. Her voice is gentle and the whites of her eyes are giant full moons. There is something quiet about her, sad and almost otherworldly. She tells me shamans act on our behalf, they are the intermediaries between our world and the spirit world, and their role is to facilitate healing. She says the worlds are interconnected and when balance is disrupted, a shaman can help restore harmony.

I lie down on a massage table with my head facing up.

"I will begin by shaking a rattle around your body and go into a trance," she says. "Then, using my hands, a feather and my breath, I will walk around you and remove any blockages of negative energy from your body. I will then add energy that is necessary for you to heal."

I close my eyes and as she rattles, I fall into a deep re-laxation, and she begins her healing. I feel the wind from her hands as they wave back and forth over my body, and she takes in short bursts of breath to remove the negative energy. Then I feel her gently blowing on the top of my head to add the healing energy.

When she is finished, and she asks me to open my eyes, I find it hard to follow this instruction. My eyes seem to be glued shut and I have to struggle to open them, as if I were in deep water, swimming up for air. As I finally get them open, she looks at me and smiles. "How are you feeling?" she asks.

"A bit slow," I respond. "But in a good way. My whole body is relaxed, as if it's made of clay."

She smiles again and nods. She tells me she has removed the blockages from my ancestors, which she found main-ly around my heart. She says there was a cloud of ancestral shame that surrounded my body and she cleared this too. She doesn't tell me what ancestral shame is but I interpret it to mean the shame of being Jewish, the shame of survival when others perished, the shame of being treated as less than, as subhuman, victimized, and the shame of feeling so burdened by this past, by all these ghosts.

She says she has removed some intrusive generational energies including being critical, judgmental and intolerant. The shaman tells me these energies were stuck in my body, causing me emotional congestion, which manifested as pain and suffering, and by removing these intrusive energies, my body should now be able to welcome joy and light. She says she has helped to protect me from these energies by filling me with inner peace, with the ability to make good decisions, to be adaptable and flexible.

"Your power animal is a butterfly," she says. "Butterflies teach lightness, brightness, joy and transformation."

When a caterpillar molts for a final time, the new skin becomes the golden chrysalis. This transformation is designed to protect the pupa until it emerges transformed into a butterfly, a complete metamorphosis. The shaman tells me that now I am reconnected with my animal totem, which will bring me strength and wisdom and teach me about joyfulness.

When we are done, I feel at peace, yet I am not ready to exit out her door back into the world.

My friend, Christie, and I are sitting in a restaurant that serves healthy food our husbands and children won't eat. Christie is having a bowl of lentil stew and I'm dipping into a tofu scramble. I butter a thick slice of rye toast and take a bite. We are talking about making art, about writing, about remembering the dead.

"Who was your great-grandmother?" Christie asks. "Who was Klára?"

Her question surprises me. I chew my toast and stare at a poster on the wall for a Kundalini yoga retreat. There is a picture of a woman sitting cross-legged, her hands in prayer by her heart. The words say something about consciousness, health and vitality.

"I don't know," I say. "I don't know much about her. Other than the fact she was a victim."

"But she was a woman," Christie says. She looks at me. Her eyes are questioning, searching, but she is smiling.

"Yes, she was," I agree. "She was both woman and victim."

Christie stirs her stew. I notice how thick it is, the pale yellow of the sweet potato.

"How could you find out more about her?" she asks.

I take a bite of toast. I can tell the bread is homemade by the unevenness of the crisp crust, the slightly sour and earthy flavour, and how dense it is. I imagine a whole loaf of this bread could weigh as much as a sack of bricks. In my family, heavy bread is good bread.

"I don't know. Everyone who knew her is dead," I say. "I do have photos. I could ask my mother again. Pick her brain."

"How old was Klára when she died?" Christie asks.

"She was fifty-nine," I say.

"Fifty-nine! That's a whole lifetime," she says. "She lived so much of her life before the war."

"It's true," I say. "I've never really thought about Klára's life before the war. It's as if her death was her defining moment."

"It's probably because the way in which she died was so horrific," Christie says. "But if she were alive today, would she tell you her life was defined by the way she died? Or would she tell you that her life was made up of what your life is made up of, what mine, what everyone's is. All her experiences, her family, her friends, her joys and fears, her heart, her breath, her body and spirit."

"Is there another way of imagining your great-grandmother?" she asks.

Is there another way of telling *her* story?

Healer #6

The way for me to heal is through my body. I need to re-connect my mind with the rest of me. I keep reading Peter Levine's writing about trauma and somatic experiencing, about a therapy designed to focus on the body and its sensations. This seemingly simple idea is quite challenging for someone like me who is so disconnected from my insides. It's actually work to notice physical sensations. When they happen I'm not aware they're even happening, because I'm so stuck in my head.

I do some research online and email a healer who practises somatic experiencing. We talk on the phone and I tell her a little bit about myself and book a session with her. Her space is in a character home, probably a hundred years old. There is a couch and a table. The room is cold and I'm not dressed properly. She tells me I can take the moss-green blanket, which sits beside me on the couch. I wrap it around my legs. The radiator clanks and she clears her throat. We smile at each other awkwardly.

"Sorry I'm late," I say. "I'm usually very punctual. I don't know what happened. I guess I just lost track of time."

"Three minutes late is not really late," she says.

"It is for me," I say.

I dive right in. A flood of words.

I talk about my labour, how I was working from a place of animal, heaving from the guts, mostly on all fours. How panicked I was when Ben's heart rate dropped, and when the first responders were called.

"Stop there," she says. "Look at your feet. See how they're moving when you tell that part of the story? They're trying to run. Let them run. This was an unfinished response to an impulse. What else are you feeling in your body?"

I close my eyes, turn inward and look.

"I'm feeling scared. I feel it in my throat all the way down through my spine and into my stomach."

"Good. Stay there. Let the sensation be there," she says.

I breathe with the panic and after a minute it begins to calm and I open my eyes. So I continue.

"They strapped me to a chair and took me down three flights of stairs into an ambulance. That's when the urge to push came on strongly. But I wasn't allowed to push because every time I did, my baby's heart would decelerate."

I'm well-rehearsed in telling this story. I usually dissociate. But when I tell it today, to this healer, I stay in my body.

"I had to fight the urge," I continue with the birth story. "I had to go against the animal."

"Okay, I'll stop you there again," she says. "Close your eyes. What are the sensations?"

"My breath is speeding up and my adrenaline is kicking in," I explain. "I'm sucking on that oxygen mask as hard as I can through the contractions. I'm so scared."

With my eyes closed, I let myself feel the sensations and I take in big gulps of air. I stay like this until the feeling dissipates and I begin to relax.

"When I got to the hospital," I continue, "there were bright lights and people running everywhere. I was screaming from the pain of contractions, of not being able to push and from fear itself. There was a nurse beside me. She yelled at me to stop screaming."

"Okay, let's pause here," she says. "An emergency nurse yelled at you to stop screaming? What did you do?"

"I listened to her," I say. "I tried to hold all of it in."

"How did that make you feel?" she asks.

"Angry," I say.

"Yes," she says. "Feel that. What does your anger look like?"

I close my eyes and go into my body. Everything is tight. I feel my hands turn into fists.

"I feel agitated. Like I want to tell her to shut up. She's leaning in close to me and I can see her spit spray as she yells. I want to punch her in the face. Okay, I'm doing it. I'm punching her in the face."

I smile and open my eyes. "That kind of felt good."

"Great," she says. "What kind of emergency nurse doesn't let a patient scream if they need to?"

"I probably triggered something in her," I say. "She couldn't handle my pain, my fear."

"Then she's obviously working in the wrong department," the healer says.

"After that I don't remember much because they put me under general anesthetic and gave me an emergency C-section. I know when they pulled my son out he wasn't breathing. His kidneys shut down. They didn't know if he'd make it. When I woke up, I was wheeled to the Neonatal Intensive Care Unit. I reached through a hole to touch Ben's hand. His body was covered in wires," I say, and tears begin to form. "I can't believe that after nine years I'm still crying," I say.

"Your sadness about Ben's birth will always be a part of who you are," the healer says.

I breathe this new information in.

"I thought it was always something I had to get rid of," I say. "That it's somehow wrong to grieve, to feel this well of sadness, so many years later. Like why can't I just get over it already?"

"Today you're looking at the birth using a different approach. Instead of just thinking about it in your mind and re-playing it that way, you're allowing the sensations into your body, letting them stay there and actually feeling them. You're allowing these sensations to complete their cycle, to have a start and a finish, instead of letting them get stuck and come out in anger," she says.

"Your body has this amazing ability to organically return to a state of equilibrium. Now what I want you to focus on is what you are sensing in your body when you're feeling good," she says.

I look at her with my mouth open, like I'm trying to register the seemingly simple thing she just said.

"It's kind of funny," I say. "I don't really pay attention to when I'm feeling good. I actually hardly ever notice it. But I really become aware when I'm not feeling good. Then it's like an obsession: Why am I feeling this way? How can I make it go away?"

She nods. "You said you're feeling good now. Let's practise. How does your body tell you it's feeling good?"

I close my eyes. I notice my breath. I search my body from the inside out. "My shoulders are down instead of up to my ears," I begin. "My heart feels open."

"How does it feel open?" she asks.

"I feel like I love the world," I say. "It's warm and there's a path leading into it and out; it flows like a river."

"Nice," she says. "Now see if you can practise that over the next couple of weeks. Remember you are rewiring your brain. It takes practice to form new pathways that your mind and body will remember. But you can do it."

I VISIT THE DOCTOR again, the one who told me not to come back until I examined my head, and I know it will be my last visit with her for quite some time. I feel a confidence in this knowing, something I haven't felt before. It feels good.

When I see her, I bring her some fancy dark chocolate. It's my way of saying thank you. Many women don't buy themselves good dark chocolate. We are too busy buying it for others. The healer opens the card and smiles. When I notice the wrinkles around her eyes, soft and warm, I feel grateful for her wisdom. This woman knows that winter is difficult for me, that I'm afraid that if I start talking I will begin to cry, that the sadness will consume me, that I will be swallowed whole.

"Have I ever told you the story of my anger?" she asks.

I shake my head no, so she tells me.

"Everyone was afraid of me," she says. "My sister called me 'The Scorpion' because I was so quick to rage, ready to whip my tail around at whomever I felt bullied by. I woke up with shaking fists, ready to fight. Finally, I got to a place where I didn't feel as though I could go on with all the anger stored within. I lit a candle and sat down. I noticed the anger rise up quickly within my body. I felt it move through me. It felt like my head was going to explode, as if I would implode. And then, just like that, the anger vanished. The next day, I sat and conjured up what little anger remained and, as I sat throughout the week, I found there wasn't any left. The anger had disappeared."

I look at her and try to picture the intensity of her anger, her scorpion tail lashing.

"You know emotion is just energy," she says. "E-motion? You get it? Energy in motion. Emotion is movement. They rise and swell like the tides."

I close my eyes and take a deep breath. A wave of energy sweeps through my body and my jaw tightens. I plant my feet firmly on the floor and wiggle my toes inside my boots.

"I think you're making great progress," she says. "Keep doing what you're doing. Create a safe space for yourself where you can feel things. Nothing changes if you don't do the work."

When I leave, I have tears in my eyes. She hugs me.

"Bah humbug," I say.

Journal Entry #93

I sit on my meditation pillow and stare out the window. Two seagulls paint the sky with their wings. The orange glow of afternoon sun makes the skyscrapers downtown look like they're on fire. It's a light that feels relaxed, warm and safe. I am doing a visualization exercise given to me by a healer who specializes in homeopathy and reconnection to the natural world. When I went to see her she told me to picture ancestral hooks detaching from my body. I close my eyes and imagine the hooks attached to trampoline springs, and to bungee cords, the kind people use to keep the trunks of their cars closed. I imagine these bungee cord hooks attaching to different internal organs. One hook on my heart, one on my lungs, my intestines, my brain. I imagine these hooks are deeply embedded into my flesh. That they won't just come out when I pull on them. That when I try and remove them, try to force them and jerk them out, they embed more deeply, like some kind of parasite that knows it's being threatened, that its time is up.

I slowly breathe in and out.

I decide to take a different approach. A gentle one. I speak to my ancestors but I don't speak out loud. I let them know that I am not here to cause them harm, that they are a part of me and always will be, that I love them. But their time in my body is finished. Their hooks aren't serving any of us. That it's time for them to let go.

I tug gently at the hooks. I imagine pulling them out, one by one. A slight jostle, an unhooking, a slow release.

Healer #7

On a Monday afternoon I drop into a dance class that is for fifty-five plus. Dancing in my living room has taught me that the energy in my body needs a place to escape. I am here as a gift to my body.

"Hi," I say to the receptionist. "Karen told me about this class. She said it would be okay for me to try it."

"You mean for free?" she asks.

"No, she said I could try it even though I'm not fifty-five. I just feel more comfortable with older people," I say.

"Got it," she says. "It's ten dollars to drop in."

I hand her the money. "Thank you," I say. "Is it in that room?" I point to the door beside the desk. The receptionist nods.

I hold my breath as I walk into the room. When I walk in, I see a young woman with long, wavy brown hair. She is speaking to an older woman with short silver hair cut into a perfect bob.

"Hi," I say. "Sorry for interrupting. I'm Claire. I came to try this class. I've never done anything like this before. Except for by myself in my living room. I'm so nervous. I'm hoping this class will be small. I heard these groups can get quite large. I'm not comfortable with crowds."

They both stare at me, smiling.

"I'm so glad you came," the younger woman says. "Welcome." She is standing behind a laptop computer. I notice her red leg warmers.

"Thanks," I say.

On the wall there are bunch of metal hooks with a bench underneath. I take off my jacket and down vest and hang them up. It has been so cold recently. A hard winter. More snow than usual. I keep my socks and my long-sleeved shirt on. The woman with the perfect bob comes and sits on the couch near the bench. The worn brown couch she sits on has a purple and green flower pattern. Next to her sits a wooden Buddha and in front of Buddha sits a double chime with a wooden mallet.

"I'm Margaret," she says. "You don't look fifty-five."

"Well, I'm almost forty and I like seniors. Does that count?" I ask.

She laughs and I notice her bangs are cut short and straight.

"Have you been here before?" I ask.

"No," she says. "First time."

I smile. "We are both being brave today," I say.

Another woman walks in, and then a man. I sit and listen to them talk about the man's recent vacation to Hawaii and how he just got back and already misses the sun. I tap my feet against the cold linoleum floor. I look over and notice the healer is fiddling with her laptop. Then the music starts. A soft, quiet, swaying beat.

"Okay," says the healer. "We're going to get started now. Can everyone gather around and we'll form a circle."

There are about eight of us. We come together to fill in the circle. We do a few warm-up exercises that involve shaking out our bodies, bending and stretching as we stand in place.

"Close your eyes," the healer says. "Let's take a few deep grounding breaths. Just let yourselves be here. Breathe in and sigh it out."

I am relieved to close my eyes, to not look at anyone else, to not see anyone else looking at me.

The music gets louder.

"Use your hands as a paintbrush," the healer says. "What colours do you see?"

My hands begin to move in small circles. As the music gets louder and faster, my circles get bigger. Soon I am painting the room in wide bursts of yellow.

After a few minutes, I open my eyes. I want to check out other people's dance moves and I don't want to bump into anyone. A woman glides by me. She has long, wavy white hair, held in place by a black headband. She wears a flowy purple tunic, cropped black pants and long feather earrings. She bends over and touches the ground and one of her legs stretches to the ceiling. It looks like she has done this before. Another man shuffles by me. He's dressed in torn jeans and a light blue polo shirt. He is more walking than dancing and he moves in straight lines, a sharp contrast to the flowy woman.

I look down at my feet. I am wearing black gym socks from Costco and my feet are moving in small steps on the green floor.

"How is your spine feeling today?" the healer asks. "Notice any sensations you're feeling in your body. If you start to drift, go back to your breath."

There are drums beating now. I focus on my spine and bend over to stretch it out. When I stand up my shoulders circle backwards. I stare up at the ceiling and pick out a cobweb on the white vent.

"Notice your hips," the healer says.

I start to sway faster and my feet lift off the floor in small hops. My body and I move across the room. My arms open and close wide, then move like snakes through the air. I notice I am smiling.

"Isn't this incredible?" the healer says. "In being here, you are choosing to honour your temple of flesh and blood and the home that you live in."

My heart swells like a balloon filled with helium and I smile through my tears. I feel like a whirling dervish and my feet barely touch the ground. I don't stop moving except for a three-second break for water. There is no thought, no sense of time, just the music and the beat and my body.

It's only when the music slows that I know we are beginning to wind down.

"Okay, everyone, let's get into our closing circle," the healer says.

We gather again, our chests heaving with breath. The nervous energy that first filled the room is gone and has been replaced with a sense of belonging, a confidence. Bodies awakened.

"Thank you for being here today and for making time for yourselves," the healer says. "I'd like to go around the circle and find a word to describe how you're feeling."

I stare hard at my feet as I listen to the words. "Relaxed." "Energized." "Present." When it's my turn I lift my head and smile.

"Grateful," I say.

August 23, 2016

Dear Ben,

I don't know when I will publish this book, nor do I know when you will come to read it. What I do know is this: Somewhere between spring and summer you shoot up two inches and your feet grow to be the same size as mine. You show me your chest and ask me if I see all the hair that is sprouting and I kiss you where your heart is and nod, pretending that I do. Your favourite food is a steaming bowl of pho or a cup of matza ball soup and you usually ask for extra noodles or matza balls. We watch musicals, *Fiddler on the Roof* and *Yentl,* and you love them just as I do. You are strong, have a mean baseball arm and I watch as the rocks you throw skip sideways across the Salish Sea.

"Let's go play-fight," you say. "You can tickle me, because it's good to laugh. Laughing makes you smarter and it's fun."

I smile because I know this is true. You are my nine-year-old teacher.

"Roll me up," you say, jumping on the bed.

You lay pin straight on the white duvet and I slowly roll you up like a burrito until your whole body is hidden. When you peek through the covers, your brown eyes flash, your plum cheeks poke out. "Hurry up and roll me. What's taking so long?" you say.

I roll you across the bed all burritoed up and swaddled. Then I open the covers where your face is and give your cherub cheeks a kiss and tickle you in the space between your chin and neck. You laugh and laugh until you get the hiccups.

"I can't breathe!" you say.

I stop and roll you until your head and half your body is falling off the bed.

"My yoga teacher taught me it's good to hang upside down," I say. "She told me it calms the nervous system and improves circulation."

You laugh more because you've heard me joke about this before. The way I push you off the bed and let you hang with the blood rushing to your brain.

"There's a dime on the floor," you say. "Pull me up."

I grab your hand and lift you until your body is on the bed and you hold up the dime.

"It's your babi," I say. "She's thinking of you."

You place the dime on my nightstand.

"Roll me up again," you say.

And I do.

Love always
Mom

WHAT DOES IT MEAN to survive? To survive while family members are being gassed and shot right in front of you? To survive being born without breath? What does it take to keep going? To continue living?

Terrence Des Pres said a survivor "is anyone who manages to stay alive in body *and* in spirit, enduring dread and hopelessness without the loss of will to carry on." There is a determination to keep going, to fight, to pull through.

There are words spoken about survivors, how they managed to keep going when all odds were against them: resilience, luck, fate, God, chance, miracle, will, spirit, faith, determination, resistance, dignity, finding meaning, inner strength, hope, chance, kindness of others.

Ultimately, there is not just one reason as to why some survived the Holocaust and some didn't. There are articles, which try and place Holocaust survivors into categories: those who were able to reconnect with their joyful spirit, and those who simply survived or didn't die. Since my grandparents weren't overly joyful people, and since no one is alive who can speak to their character before and during the war, these sorts of articles leave me feeling angry, because obviously I would have preferred my grandparents be in the category of those survivors who were able to find both an outward and inner *joie de vivre*. These articles fail to address the thousands who survived and had difficulty finding joy amidst the pain of their individual and collective traumas. The experience of each survivor, before, during and after the war, remains so vastly different. That some survivors expressed more joy than others post-war does not in fact make them more successful as people, nor does it make their descendants any more resilient.

As Des Pres said, the identity of a survivor includes the dead. My grandparents carried the weight of their family and friends who were murdered, the weight of not being able to live the life they wanted, the weight of years they had lost, and then my grandmother carried the weight of my grandfather's suicide. My mother carries these stories and she passed them to me, and I have passed some to my son, along with his own birth story, the one that he survived.

For some survivors, and the generations following, part of the journey of survival, and ultimately of healing, includes the telling and retelling of stories. We carry these stories inside ourselves. When we are ready, we can share these stories, write them down, an act of bearing witness to our survival. This telling of our stories is also a way of healing our wounds. As we tell our stories and share them, we work through our trauma. As we give our testimony and process our grief, we are able to create meaning, as psychiatrist and Holocaust survivor Viktor Frankl said. And although the trauma will continue to be a part of us, once we share it, we make room for new narratives to form.

Journal Entry #99

I don't try to imagine what Klára's life was like. It doesn't feel right. In fact, it feels false, like I'd be doing her a disservice, that I'd somehow be doing an injustice to her memory. I stick to the facts—so I don't get caught up in the horrific way she died, and so I can keep remembering she lived a life before herdeath.

A list of things I know about my Klára:

1. Klára Kaufmannova was born in 1883 in Jistebnice, a small town in South Bohemia.
2. Klára and Vilém were married in 1906. Vilém was born in 1870 in the small village of Pricovy in South Bohemia. He was thirteen years older than Klára. Vilém wanted to wait until his sisters were all married before he and Klára wed.
3. Klára was twenty-eight when my babi was born on December 18, 1911. This is the same age my mother was when she had me. When Ben was born, I had just turned twenty-nine.
4. My great-grandparents rented a small apartment on Karlova Street in the Old Town of Prague. Karlova Street connects the Charles Bridge with the Old Town. The apartment building is still there. It's beige and three stories tall. Like many old streets in Prague, there are cobblestones and it's narrow and winding. Today, Karlova Street is filled with tourists and souvenir shops.
5. On October 27, 1914, Klára gave birth to Richard.
6. From this apartment, Vilém would walk to work at his wholesale textile business. Klára would stay home to care for the children. When she was older, my babi worked as a bookkeeper at her father's store.
7. Klára and Vilém had a housekeeper and a cook who spoke German and French so the children could learn languages.
8. My babi told my mother that Klára was kind and well-liked.
9. Large family gatherings would be held at their summer home in Radešovice. Babi and Richard would play together with their cousins next door, hunt for mushrooms, swim in the lake and pick fruit from the gardens.

August 29, 2016

Dear Ben,

I am learning to stand upright. I know that might sound funny. But it's true. I never knew how to walk in the world with my head held high. The result of years of hunching over is a curved spine, stiff vertebrae, tight pelvis, glutes, calves, ankles and feet. A bunion forms on my left foot. The left side of my body is tighter than my right. My heart sits in the middle but tilts to the left.

I never listened to my body, never knew to tune in, never heard it when it spoke to me. Until it was too late. Until my problems became chronic. I could have listened to my adrenals when they spoke to me—the two dull spots of pain throbbing on my lower back just above my kidneys, as I rushed to get to an appointment with my baby strapped into his car seat. "Please don't cry. Please don't cry. Can we just make it to your appointment without you crying."

I could have listened to my shoulders as they flew up to my ears and stayed there, my back tight, vertebrae glued together like tectonic plates that continue to collide and fuse instead of gently gliding around.

I should have listened to my ovaries, to my uterus, telling me to "slow-the-fuck-down." But I had a baby to take care of. I had to make sure I kept him alive.

I should have listened to my nervous system, the one that works double overtime seven days a week, the one I have allowed to deplete me, the one that has caused my hormones to derail.

I should have listened to my body when I pushed those tidal waves of rage and grief back down. Because those waves always come back up.

Every crack and creak my body makes is a warning. I know this now. I am starting to pay attention. To listen.

You know that song, the one that goes, "Your toe bone connected to your foot bone, your foot bone connected to your ankle bone," and then it continues all the way up to your head? Well, it's true. Everything *is* connected. When one thing is off, everything goes. My body wants to heal. I can feel it growing stronger. I hear it now. I am listening.

I still have PMDD and I'm still hypothyroid. My hormones are still wacky and I still have a nervous system that won't stop. And yet.

And yet I can feel something is shifting. My back isn't holding as much tension. My body isn't as tight. I feel lighter.

I am listening.

Learning to stand upright is like an unfolding.

A fiddlehead begins to unfurl in spring and marks the end of winter. When I stand upright, I notice how I can look people in the eye. I am strong enough to meet a gaze and hold it there for a second without dying. I am retraining my body. I am letting it know that it is safe. That I exist. That it's okay to take up space.

In the spring I learn how to walk upright.

Love always,
Mom

MY BOSOM FRIEND CHRISTIE invites me over to make art in her studio. She has been encouraging me to use a photo of Klára in my project. When she first suggested this, I didn't think I could. I keep the photos my mother gave me of our family inside envelopes, which are inside a box, which is inside my bedroom closet. I don't look at them. It's too difficult.

It took me six months to warm up to Christie's idea. In that time, something had shifted in me. Although I still keep the photos in the box, I am able to look at them without the same stab of fear. I choose a photo of Klára sitting in a chair. It's the one where I can see my babi's features etched on her face. The one in which I picture myself as a child, sitting on the carpet by her feet, Klára in a rocking chair, sharing her secrets with me. In the black and white photo she is around fifty. Her hair is parted to the side and falls to her ears in soft waves. She leans back in her chair, half smiling, as if on the edge of a you-had-to-be-there kind of laugh. Her eyes seem to follow me: "Let me tell you a story," they say. She is wearing small, studded earrings. Around her neck is a string of pearls and over her shoulders, a diamond-patterned silk scarf. Her dress has triangle cut-outs along the V-neck and is embroidered down the middle. Her sleeves are sheer and she wears a bracelet that could be gold with jewels. There is a broach pinned to the right side of her chest.

The walls of Christie's art studio are full of her brilliant collages and paintings made by her kids. There are three bookcases, and a small blue loveseat sits next to a piano. The walls are terra cotta and avocado green and the ceiling is painted a Provençal blue. A brown armoire is tucked into one corner and I notice a yoga mat rolled up on the floor. Her desk is made out of an old French door and I can see rose petals strewn inside the glass. On her desk is a computer and a bouquet of ranunculus mixed with salal. Pens, felts, pencil crayons and pastels are lined up neatly in different holders.

There is a candle that is lit and the room smells like vanilla and chai spice. Through the sliding door, I can see outside to her backyard: green grass and forest.

I hand Christie the photo of Klára and she scans it, and I watch as my great-grandmother magically appears on the computer screen. Christie fiddles with the size and colour and then presses print. I take the printed image of Klára and walk over to the stand-up desk. I have brought a nine-by-thirteen inch wooden canvas. Christie had asked me a series of questions before we began this project. One question was about which colour I associated with Klára. I wasn't supposed to think about it. Instead I closed my eyes and felt my heart. I chose violet. Later, I do a Google search and learn that violet is the colour of transformation. A colour that can help with grief and stress and is linked with spiritual growth.

Christie turns on some soft acoustic singer-songwriter music. I begin to tear the violet paper and glue it down to the wood. Christie walks me through it and stands beside me for support. I am nervous. I want to honour Klára. I don't want to fail.

"Klára wouldn't have expected it to be perfect," she says. "You're doing great. Keep going."

I paint over the paper using a mix of antique rose and ivory and gently smudge the paint with a wet wipe. I glue an image of Prague, of Karlova Street, where Klára used to live. And then I glue the picture of Klára. In deep purple ink I stamp the word "Remember" underneath her photo. I add sparkly dimensional pink cherry blossom stickers.

"She'd look good with one in her hair," says Christie, sticking a flower in Klára's waves.

"She does look happy," I say.

I remove the flower but then put it back in her hair. Then I take it off again and leave it with the other stickers. I check my phone for the time.

"It's okay to set your artwork aside," says Christie. "You don't need to finish it in one day. Sometimes giving things space can be helpful."

I nod in agreement. Part of this project includes the cutting and pasting of words. But I don't know what I want to write yet and it's time to pick up Ben from school.

"Thank you, my friend," I say.

She walks over where I am putting my supplies away in a box and gives me a big hug.

"You're so welcome," she says.

Later, when I bring the artwork home, I lean it up against the wall. The one that overlooks my desk where I write. Klára watches over me as I type; she leans over my shoulder, guides me. I can feel her presence, and when I turn around to look at her, she is there, smiling at me.

August 31, 2016

Dear Ben,
Having you helped me to open my eyes wide enough to realize something needed to change. That *I* needed to change. I
didn't want you to learn my anger. Didn't want to keep beating
myself up. If I wanted to break my family's pattern, I needed
to learn how to calm my agitated nervous system.

Through my dear friend Linda, I learned about meditation. I started to practise sitting meditation and studied Bud-
dhist teachings, about slowing things down, about kindness
to self and to others. After a few months of practice and with
the guidance of healers and friends, I watched as the walls
around my heart began to crumble.

I was crafting a new story for myself.

I will always carry the stories of my family. They are a
part of me, of you. But do I simply keep going, getting caught
in the same patterns, the same suffering, or do I, as Lidia
Yuknavitch says, "Go down to the dark place and bring something worthwhile back"?

What if, as we continue to work through our stories, we
form new narratives, or as Yuknavitch says, "Make up stories
until you find one you can live with."

We don't have to stay stuck. We can create new paths for
ourselves. We have a choice in how we live our lives, and with
whom we share them with. If we don't like something, we can
change it.

Love always,
Mom

I DON'T BELIEVE THERE IS ONE ANSWER or one solution to anything. Often, working through trauma is harder than not working through it. But in the long run, I know that if I don't work through my pain, if I don't go to those most feared places, life will be harder for me. There will be more suffering. There will be more pain. *And it could kill me.* It was only when I was ready to go to those dark places that healing could begin.

Making sense of the horrific isn't possible, but making meaning from a traumatic experience is. I won't be able to understand the genocide, the murder of my family members, the suffering of my grandparents, the magnitude of loss, but I am trying to tell their stories. Even if only in fragments. Even if I have to imagine the places between what I know. Even when my imagination fails me and I must find other ways of remembering.

Viktor Frankl wrote about creating meaning in life despite hardship and suffering. That instead of feeling despair, we can rise above ourselves, a transcendence of the self, and turn our personal tragedies into triumphs. We may not be able to change the fact that we are suffering, but we can adjust our attitude to it.

There is love. There is beauty. There is art. There is helping others.

When I remember my ancestors, the story of my grandparents who survived, along with the stories of those who perished, it will be with a new narrative. One that isn't haunted by ghosts, that isn't burdened with the horror of the past, of trauma, victimization and death, or laden with images of smokestacks or striped prison uniforms. I would like more than anything for the cycle to have been broken with me, the third generation. Although I can't control the generational transmission of trauma, I can tell Ben's birth story and my family's story in a new way.

The new narrative is this: that both of these stories are narratives of survival and the continuity of life.

It's a new way of thinking for me, one that will require re-hardwiring of my brain. Like many people, my neurons and synapses fire repeatedly and attach themselves to largely negative stories. These stories play over and over in my head, much in the way that the media picks up on a horrific news item and the TV screen flashes the same disturbing images for days, even weeks, sometimes months.

There are those who think changing one's own brain pathways is impossible. But research is showing the opposite to be true. There are many studies that show it's possible to change how we think and how we react.

In his book *Hardwiring Happiness*, neuropsychologist Rick Hanson says people can grow new neural circuits in their brains by taking in and staying with positive experiences. Resting the mind on a positive experience allows it to install in the brain.

In *Childhood Disrupted*, science journalist Donna Jackson Nakazawa tells us there are ways of reversing epigenetic changes. That our brains have the capacity to heal themselves.

If we can help shape our brains to a certain extent, then we are not what our past tells us we are, we are more. We will always carry these stories with us but we aren't only our past, we aren't only these stories.

We are more.

Building a new story for myself will take a lifetime, and it includes so much pain, but it also brings about brilliant joy, and in this unfolding I am awakening, freeing myself and opening up to life's creative forces. Instead of feeling shame about my ancestors, my family, my history, I feel grateful. I feel thankful that I am here, and I am here because of them. I'm no longer embarrassed by my past, no longer see it as a weakness, a curse, something to overcome. I can see it now as a source of strength, a powerful force, flowing deep from within my body.

My ancestors are reminding me to go and live my life. That it's through living and remembering and grieving and living and grieving and remembering that we share our stories, that I can share them with Ben.

In the quiet of a collective whisper, my ancestors speak to me: *Don't forget to come back to the light.*

Journal Entry #100

It's Yom HaShoah, Holocaust Remembrance Day. The blossoms are so thick on the cherry trees that I can no longer see the branches. The spring sun is out and there are only a few wisps of clouds. In the Granville Island Market, I scan the buckets of flowers. I'm scouting for wild-looking ones: beach peas, delphinium, lilies, poppies, sweet clover, bleeding heart. I spot some anemones. They're red. I choose them in memory of the blood that was spilled. I choose them to honour my family. Anemones grow wild. I picture them spreading over a grassy field that covers the mass graves of my ancestors.

I pay $12.99 for a small bunch of these flowers.

"Is this a gift or are they going home today?" the florist asks.

I pause. "Um," I seem to say forever. My eyes go fuzzy and I stare at the counter. Hard.

"I think they're for me," I answer. "For home."

"Don't put too much water in the vase, as they're a soft-stemmed flower," she says. "This will prevent them from rotting."

I want to tell her that I'll be cutting them up. But I don't. I thank her and I leave.

Outside the market, seagulls with fat bellies waddle by the garbage container, looking for scraps. One finds a take-out container with leftover French fries and two others wander over. A fight breaks out and the biggest bird wins. I watch the seagull guzzle the fries whole, and fly off, crying out its song of victory.

When I return home to our apartment, I Google and learn anemones are used for their medicinal properties in the treatment of menstrual problems and grief. I am a firm believer that our bodies know how to heal themselves. We simply need to learn how to tune in.

I place the larger photos of my great grandparents along with my babi's brother, Richard, on the wood table. Below, I place photos of my grandparents, and my great-aunt and her family. There's even a family photo of my great-great-grandmother. Her name was Josefa. She sits outside on a white wicker chair. There is a cherry tree, plums, apples and pears. The grass is long and there are daisies. She is dressed in black. A large-collared, long-sleeved blouse and a skirt that flows down to her ankles. Her grey hair is pulled back away from her face. She holds her left hand in her right. She wears a ring on her right ring finger. She's smiling and her four family members are standing behind her, smiling too. My Klára, my Vilém, my babi, and my Richard. I don't understand how the photos survived, when most of my family didn't. I am, however, grateful to have them.

Next to the photos sits a typed list of names of our family members, and the anemones I cut at the top of the stalk. Beside the flowers, there is water sitting in a stainless steel bowl. I clear my throat. I am nervous even though it's just the three of us. Ben and Jeremy look at me expectantly.

I begin to speak about the Holocaust. I talk about how most members of our family were murdered, but I don't mention details. I speak about how my babi and děda survived, and that we are here because of them. And I talk about how we must remember, how we must always remember. Then I turn to the photos.

"Here's your great-great-grandmother," I say.

Ben grabs an anemone. He is ready to start. I hold up the photo of my Klára, my namesake, and take a deep breath.

"Dear Klára," I say. My voice box begins to shake. "We love you and we will always remember you."

Ben watches me and I nod to him. He places the anemone in the bowl of water. The three of us watch the red drift in the silver bowl.

We continue through the photos. We are learning how to grieve, practising how to mourn together. We are creating a ritual to make our own.

I hold up the photo of my grandmother.

"That's Babi," Ben says.

I smile at him through my tears.

"Dear Babi," I say. "We love you and we will always remember you."

Ben puts another anemone into the bowl.

We do another one for my děda and then we do some for Jeremy's side of the family. He doesn't have photos but he has a long list of names.

When we are done, there is so much red in the bowl that I can't see any water.

We take the elevator down and we walk behind the building where there is a line of trees near a pond.

"What tree do you think would be best?" I ask.

Ben looks around. He points to a cherry, the one in the middle, its blossoms like pink snowflakes. I place a hand on the bark.

"This is good tree," I say.

Jeremy puts the bowl near the tree's roots. Then one by one the three of us place the anemones around the base of the trunk. When we are all finished, Ben empties the bowl of water on the roots, back into the earth.

We look at each other and the three of us link arms. The tree looks beautiful. We walk back this way, all woven up together.

"Mom?" Ben says.

"Hmm?" I reply.

"Is your book about me?" he asks.

"Yes," I say.

September 1, 2016

Dear Ben,

I am hiking alone on Channel Ridge on Salt Spring Island, a three-hour ferry ride from Vancouver. We have moved out of the city to be closer to nature. To slow down. To build community. To play. We moved here for you.

The trail is steep at first and I am already out of breath and sweating. There is salal, fern and Oregon grape. Cedar, Douglas fir, hemlock and big leaf maple. I am stepping on a mess of needles, leaves, small rocks, dirt and tree roots. The bright green moss looks like shag carpet. My favourite kind of hike. There is a dead tree covered in woodpecker holes; its trunk sticks up sharp where it snapped and fell over.

I hike up another hill and come to a forest of arbutus. The trees are twisted, hunched over as if disfigured from trauma. Yet these trees are strong, able to withstand windstorms and drought.

I come to a clearing that has a bench. It is dedicated to a man who supported the opening of this trail system. There is a view of the Salish Sea and beyond this, Vancouver Island. I can hear the hum of the ferry unloading at Vesuvius terminal below.

In the clearing there is an arbutus tree unlike any other I've seen. It's massive, and its branches stretch east searching for the morning sun. The top layer of bark looks like old roof shingle. Under this, a thin second layer, rusty coloured like blood—it curls when it's peeled away. In the third layer, its skin is revealed: red, orange and yellows, warm colours, flesh.

There is no bark on one of its branches and it juts out, low, like a giant arm, naked and smooth. An outline of a heart carved long ago, "MB + DS." I massage the tree's skin and feel the familiar tightening of my jaw, the wet in the corner of my eyes. I lean my forehead against the tree's bare arm. It feels cool against my skin and I can feel the hot summer sun on the back of my neck. My hands are open, relaxed, pulsing with blood. I look up and do a small back bend, heart out, face up, to witness this gift, to stand in the shadow of this tree's beauty, its magnificence, arms by my sides, strong in mountain pose, I call to my ancestors, "Here I am."

Love always,
Mom

BIBLIOGRAPHY

Berceli, David, Ph.D. *Tension Releasing Exercises.* (Pamphlet), 1998.

Des Pres, Terrence. *The Survivor: An Anatomy of Life in the Death Camps.* Oxford: Oxford University Press, 1976.

Epstein, Helen. *Where She Came From: A Daughter's Search For Her Mother's History.* New York: Little, Brown and Company, 1997.

Frank, Anne. *Anne Frank: The Diary of a Young Girl.* New York: Bantam Books, 1993.

Frankl, Victor E. *Man's Search for Meaning.* Boston: Beacon Press, 2006.

Hanson, Rick, Ph.D. *Hardwiring Happiness: The New Brain Science of Contentment, Calm, and Confidence.* New York: Harmony Books, 2013.

Hirsch, Marianne. *The Generation of Postmemory: Writing and Visual Culture after the Holocaust.* New York: Columbia University Press, 2012.

Jilovsky, Esther, Jordana Silverstein, and David Slucki, eds. *In the Shadows of Memory: The Holocaust and the Third Generation.* London: Vallentine Mitchell, 2016.

Kellermann, Natan P.F. *Holocaust Trauma: Psychological Effects and Treatment.* Indiana: iUniverse, 2009.

Kovály, Heda Margolius. *Under a Cruel Star: A Life in Prague 1941–1968.* New York: Penguin Books, 1989.

Ledgerwood, Angela. *Lit up* interview: "Chapter 15: The Way Forward with Lidia Yuknavitch." Podcast audio. July 21, 2015. soundcloud.com/litupshow/chapter-15-shedding-tears-with-lidia-yuknavitch

Levi, Primo. *Survival in Auschwitz: The Nazi Assault on Humanity.* New York: Touchstone, 1996.

Levine, Peter A. *Trauma and Memory: Brain and Body in a Search for the Living Past.* Berkeley: North Atlantic Books, 2015.

Levine, Peter A. *Waking The Tiger: Healing Trauma.* California: North Atlantic Books, 1997.

Nakazawa, Donna Jackson. *Childhood Disrupted: How Your Biography Becomes Your Biology, And How You Can Heal.* New York: Atria Books, 2015.

Pisano, Nirit Gradwohl. *Granddaughters of the Holocaust: Never Forgetting What They Didn't Experience.* Brighton: Academic Studies Press, 2012.

Rosensaft, Menachem Z., ed. *God, Faith & Identity from the Ashes: Reflections of Children and Grandchildren of Holocaust Survivors.* Vermont: Jewish Lights Publishing, 2015.

Tippett, Krista. *On Being* interview with Rachel Yehuda, Ph.D.: "How Trauma and Resilience Cross Generations." Podcast audio. July 30, 2015. soundcloud.com/onbeing/rachel-yehuda-how-trauma-and-resilience-cross-generations.

Van der Kolk, Bessel, M.D. *The Body Keeps Score: Brain, Mind, and Body in the Healing of Trauma.* New York: Penguin Books, 2014.

Weisel, Mindy, ed. *Daughters of Absence: Transforming a Legacy of Loss.* Illinois: Dream of Things, 2012.

Wolynn, Mark. *It Didn't Start With You: How Inherited Family Trauma Shapes Who We Are and How to End the Cycle.* New York: Viking, 2016.

Yuknavitch, Lidia. *The Chronology of Water: A Memoir.* Portland: Hawthorne Books & Literary Arts, 2010.

Yuknavitch, Lidia. *Writing & The Body.* A workshop held in Ojai, September 2015.

ACKNOWLEDGMENTS

Thank you to everyone who held me throughout the making of this book.

Thank you to Vici Johnstone, Michael Despotovic and everyone at Caitlin Press for believing in my work, and for continuing to put themselves out there fearlessly by publishing books by authors whose voices might not otherwise be heard.

A big, heaping heart thanks to Sarah Schantz, whose brilliant editing eyes helped make magic on the pages.

To Ruth Daniell, a huge thank you for your edits and for holding my hand through the final push.

To my dear friend Dr. Abby Wener Herlin, thank you for your constant support, your generosity and guidance.

Thank you to Dr. Robert Krell for your words of wisdom. I am so grateful.

To my bosom friend Christie Roome, thank you for making art with me and for helping me shift my perspective in such a life-changing way.

I am eternally grateful to Lidia Yuknavitch and Jennifer Pastiloff for opening their hearts, making space, and bearing witness to the creative energies that come from being vulnerable.

Thank you to everyone at Humber School for Writers.

Thank you to writers extraordinaire: Emily Klein, Danielle Hubbard, Dawn Leonard, Linda Quennec, Laura Scappaticci, Ellen Schwartz, Jennifer Stanic, and the fierce women of Ojai Ovary.

To Shirley, Ted, Daniel and Frank, thank you for all your encouragement.

Thank you to all our friends on Salt Spring Island for welcoming us to your rock.

To my mom, who journeyed along with me and never wavered from entering the dark places. I can't thank you enough for being so brave, for telling your story, and for giving me permission to set it free.

To my dad and sister, thank you for putting up with me.

To the loves of my life, Jeremy and Ben, I wouldn't be here without either of you. I love you so much.

And to my ancestors, whose voices will continue to live in me and who I will always remember.

PHOTO: RAMONA LAM

CLAIRE SICHERMAN is a graduate of the creative non-fiction program at The Humber School for Writers. Her work has appeared in the anthology *Sustenance: Writers from B.C. and Beyond on the Subject of Food*, and on Zathom.com. She lives with her husband and son on Salt Spring Island, British Columbia.